CREATING A THRIVING FAMILY BUSINESS

CREATING A THRIVING FAMILY BUSINESS
Progress Not Perfection

John Broons

'This book is essential reading for every family business. John's fireside chat style weaves a story that demystifies the complexity of a family business and illuminates a pathway to prosperity. It will help get the whole family on the same page – a great foundation for building a successful, resilient family business.'

Steve Samson, former Director of Sadliers Transport (established 1829) and past National President of Family Business Association

'John Broons has spent his life in and around family businesses. His passion for these organisations – and the people inside them – shines through in this book. John's experience and wisdom come through in every chapter of *Creating a Thriving Family Business*. It's a wonderful guide for anyone on the family business journey.'

Jerry Kleeman, CEO and Director, Kleeman International

'Love the stages. It's easy to read, insightful, and full of practical advice that will resonate with many families in business together.'

Paul Andrews, Founder, Family Business United

'John's intimate writing style makes this book a joy to read – it's as if he's speaking directly to you. The book is packed with practical wisdom about what it really takes to build and sustain a successful family business, and as we all know, common sense isn't all that common – so this one's a keeper! John strikes a thoughtful balance between the emotional dynamics of "familyness" – particularly communication and trust – and a clear, practical blueprint that covers shared values, charters and succession planning. His personal anecdotes and real-world reflections bring the content to life and make it deeply relatable.'

Dr Steven Dorevitch

'This book is like sitting down with someone who's seen it all – and actually cares. John Broons doesn't sugarcoat the challenges of running a family business, but he also doesn't make it sound impossible. His stories are real, his advice is practical, and the whole thing is built around helping families work better together, not just run a better business. If you're part of a family business, this book will give you clarity, confidence, and a few "aha" moments you didn't expect. It's not about perfection – it's about progress. And that's exactly what makes it so useful.'

Harry Kras, family business consultant and founding director, Family Business Resource Centre

For my grandparents, my parents, my wonderful wife, my children, their partners, and my grandchildren. My beautiful family.

First published in 2025 by John Broons
www.johnbroons.com

© John Broons 2025
The moral rights of the author have been asserted

All rights reserved. Except as permitted under the *Australian Copyright Act 1968* (for example, a fair dealing for the purposes of study, research, criticism or review), no part of this book may be reproduced, stored in a retrieval system, communicated or transmitted in any form or by any means without prior written permission. No part of this book may be used or reproduced in any manner for the purpose of training artificial intelligence technologies or systems.

All inquiries should be made to the author.

A catalogue entry for this book is available from the National Library of Australia.

Printed in Australia by Pegasus
Book production and text design by Publish Central
Cover design by Julia Kuris

The paper this book is printed on is certified as environmentally friendly.

Disclaimer: The material in this publication is of the nature of general comment only, and does not represent professional advice. It is not intended to provide specific guidance for particular circumstances and it should not be relied on as the basis for any decision to take action or not take action on any matter which it covers. Readers should obtain professional advice where appropriate, before making any such decision. To the maximum extent permitted by law, the author and publisher disclaim all responsibility and liability to any person, arising directly or indirectly from any person taking or not taking action based on the information in this publication.

CONTENTS

Welcome		1
Step 1	**Unite:** the key to creating a thriving enterprise	29
Step 2	**Build:** align your family with the business	59
Step 3	**Transition:** from one generation to the next	95
Your legacy		123
Appendix	Workbook: if you were hit by a bus	127
Why work with a family business adviser?		145
The six-month program for small family businesses		147
The 12-month program for large family businesses		149
Individual coaching		151
If you're looking for a speaker ...		153

*'The elevator to success is out of order.
You'll have to take the stairs ... one step at a time.'*

Joe Girard, world's greatest salesman
(Guinness World Records)

WELCOME

'Time is not your enemy. It will give you clarity.'
John Broons

Thank you for choosing to read this book about families running businesses.

You are appreciated. More than you realise.

You'll notice the title: *Creating a Thriving Family Business: Progress not Perfection*.

The name is not just another book title. It is a philosophy.

There has never been a perfect business. Nor has there ever been a perfect family.

To the outside world, a family can *seem* perfect – much like a business.

But the opposite is usually true.

A family is like a tapestry: the outside world sees a beautiful picture woven from thousands of threads of many colours, while the reverse of the tapestry can look chaotic, with no clarity, form or function.

Progress to a better situation. This book is not about doom and gloom.

There'll be no hyperbole about the unmitigated disaster awaiting you, your family or your business if you don't subscribe to my all-knowing wisdom.

I'm not a guru or a saviour. This is not the six steps to untold riches.

But there *are* steps for you to take to progress to a better situation for your family business. Steps to transition from one generation to the next.

Three of them, to be exact.

The steps are about bringing the family who runs the business together, so that the family can use a business to achieve their goals.

Ultimately, I want your family to do well, and for each member of the family to do well. So each individual is free to set their course, while hopefully aligning behind a business that supports everyone. Where each individual family member chooses to be involved with the family business – or not. Whether that be working in it, working on it, or simply owning part of it – or not.

Family first, business second

I like to see myself as both an interested and compassionate guide. Someone who, from a very young age, was exposed to (our) family business. Someone who liked what I saw – even then – and who has now spent the better part of my six or more decades on earth working on, with and for family-owned businesses like yours.

My philosophy is *family first, business second*.

I don't advise on business challenges without considering the family who is challenged.

I believe in uniting the family behind the business, to ensure they can build the business to achieve their goals, and

ultimately, with those foundations in place, transition the business from generation to generation – to not only survive, but flourish and thrive.

Family is important to me. I am part of the third generation of a family that owned and operated a business which has transformed through the generations from a diverse publicly listed corporation in my youth, to a privately owned business as a young adult, to one that I managed with my sister before transitioning again to owning and operating my own business and then transitioning to my current role as a family business adviser.

Our family has gathered around the dinner table for generations to enjoy each other's company – although not always – to talk about business plans – not agreeing every time – and to share our lives – in good times and bad.

I know what it is like to revere a grandfather – Poppa – who was beloved in the family and by staff and the wider community. I know what it is like to chafe against the direction of my father when I had ideas I wanted to implement into the family business. I know what it is like to be overlooked for a position that I wanted – even though I may not have been the best qualified. I know what it is like to lose the head of the family business, and I've experienced the chaotic times that resulted from those events.

Combined with my work with many family-owned businesses over the years, I have drawn on conversations with first-, second-, third- and even fourth-generation family members who owned or operated the family business. Helping dads pass on a business to sons. Helping daughters navigate decisions made by their parents that they found difficult to understand. Helping siblings decide if and where they wanted to be involved in the transition of a business from their parents.

The challenges of family business

I've seen and experienced enough to know the lay of the land. I deeply appreciate families who run businesses. I value the opportunity to help them.

Every family business is unique – and so are the people in it. I've had the privilege of working with families in all kinds of situations: some straightforward, others more complex. These next few stories highlight just how different the journey can be, and why listening, patience and a bit of flexibility often matter more than any formal plan.

One said yes, one said no

In one situation, Mum and Dad wanted to exit, and there were two boys who could potentially come into the business and take it over. One of the boys had strong financial skills and the other was quite business savvy. In this instance, one of the boys wanted to come into the business and the other didn't. It was a relatively simple decision for both of them, and the transition was able to occur under those circumstances.

This story shows how a simple, honest conversation can lead to a clean and effective transition. When everyone's clear on what they want, things don't have to be complicated.

Trying to do the right thing

In another business, the father invited me into a very successful business. When I started talking to them, it was just about bringing the family together for the first time in a family meeting. Now Mum knew everyone in the business; she was the one who organised the birthday cakes for every birthday. They had some other family members in executive positions, and they were very good at what they did. There were sons and daughters who were good at what they did.

Now, without going into all the gory details, it was only the first meeting when one of the sons got up and left, with a few choice parting words. It turned out he had a drug problem, and Dad was trying to do the right thing by bringing him back into the business, but it really wasn't the right thing to do, and the family had a lot of issues to cope with in that situation.

The intent of the owners doesn't always carry through. The next generation has to want to be there. And siblings don't always get along.

This case highlights the risks of assuming good intentions are enough. Without addressing deeper issues, even well-meaning plans can unravel – and sometimes the hardest part is accepting what's really best for the family.

Dad had a plan, but they had their own ideas

A businessman invited me in to help with the transition of the family business. He had seven daughters and three sons. There was no direction about the daughters – the father said, 'Don't worry, they'll be taken care of in a different way.'

I met with the three boys over about six months and we discussed the business and how a transition would occur. I discussed how the dad wanted each boy to buy one-third of the business and join the business, and the process he had designed for each of the boys to follow.

After about six months of bi-weekly education, each of the three boys had their own epiphany and said they understood what their dad wanted them to do.

Dad had basically instructed that each boy was to go and get his qualifications and then come back and buy into the business.

But it was Dad's plan, and as it turned out, the boys understood, but in the subsequent few months, two of the boys decided they didn't want to buy in, and only one son decided to proceed. He bought the entire business from his dad and is doing quite well.

This is a good example of working through the process and allowing individuals to decide for themselves what they want their role to be. Two decided not to become part of the family business and it was a good outcome for all concerned. Dad might have been a little disappointed, but in the end, it worked out.

Brothers-in-law

One business I worked with was started by a couple of people who'd left their profession to open up their own business. After a few years, one of the partners decided to go overseas and work in England with his wife.

During this time, the partner who stayed in Australia fell in love with his business partner's sister, they married, and this made them brothers-in-law.

At some point, the business started to struggle. One partner was making money overseas, the other wasn't. So the partner and brother-in-law in England put some extra money into the business, but that didn't solve the issues.

The overseas couple returned and the partners began working together again, but after a while, the partner and his wife who had put money in said, 'We want our money back out' – but there was no cash to take out.

Guess what? Nothing was recorded, no agreement, no documentation, and no money in a business that was still failing, and of course this strained both the business and the relationships – which were now both business and family relationships.

Father and son
In another business, the son was working in the business with his dad, who retired but kept ownership of parts of the business. The son wanted to get Dad out of the business but didn't have the cash to buy him out. This was an exercise over time to help Dad realise he had something of value and to be willing to exit, while also ensuring the son was being coached to take the time to do it right. In this case, he was doing a great job running the business but also had to work through the transition to owning it.

What's mine isn't yours
Another challenge was a sibling who had left the family business to start his own enterprise. Unfortunately, he wasn't doing well, and his mum had been supporting him. But then he went and took money from his mum's account without her knowledge. I had to help the siblings navigate this difficult situation.

Surprise, surprise
I had worked with a family business for some months when, in one meeting, I was surprised by a sudden eruption from one third-generation family member who stood up and basically told a parent he wouldn't be sad when they died. This called for a time-out. There was no indication of this animosity in our earlier conversations.

Family roast
I had a beautiful relationship with another family and we'd invested a lot of time putting together family values, agreements

and other plans for the business. As a thank you, I was invited to join them for their regular family roast on a Sunday.

It was a lovely time, and we enjoyed each other's company, but in a stunning coda, I received a call the next morning that Dad had had a heart attack overnight and was in hospital.

The good news is he is alive and well, but thank goodness we'd spent the time to put all the family ducks in a row, as the outcome could have been so different, as it has for many families where a key owner and family member passes away without the plans and organisation having been done, or key elements of the business being in the head of the owner and documented nowhere else.

You didn't ask me

Father and daughter work in the business together, and things are going well. It is accepted that the daughter will at some point take over the family business from Dad. Everyone is happy with that.

At a certain point, Dad hires his brother-in-law to take on a specific role. He does a great job and becomes a key part of the business's success.

One day, out of nowhere and without discussing anything with his daughter – the future owner of the business – Dad decides to give 10% of the business to him.

Well, something hit the fan, as you would expect.

It took a bit of work, but in the end, I had to get Dad to roll back his offer, and the brother-in-law left the business, but the outcome could have been much worse.

This is a great example of thinking through the consequences of ownership and how it relates to operations. Dad would have been far better off asking his daughter first or rewarding his brother-in-law's performance and impact in some other way rather than with shares.

Why family-owned businesses are important

Of course, I'm sure you already recognise the importance of your business to your family. Although, on more than one occasion, you have probably asked if it is all worthwhile.

I've already shared why family business is important to me. I also want to share a few facts about why family-owned businesses are important to our community, economy and country.

This is a view that is perhaps uniquely Australian, but it is by no means parochial, and my experience has been that family business is important to the economy of many countries in Asia, Europe and the Americas. As such, while my facts and figures might be uniquely Australian, the concept of family business is not unique to Australia.

Family business in Australia

The statistics don't lie.

There are over 2.5 million businesses in Australia. Over 90% of these are either sole traders or micro businesses. Together, SMEs – up to 200 employees – contribute between 30% and 40% of our entire GDP.

Fully 70% of all businesses in Australia are family-owned. That is more than 1.75 million enterprises.

These businesses employ over half of the entire Australian workforce.

As we get older, those who stay in the workforce are increasingly likely to be associated with a family business. About 13% of all workers aged over 70 are working in a family business.

Among those over 80, it rises to 24% of all workers being a contributing family worker.

This emphasises the longevity of family, as well as the fact that the transition of family businesses can be delayed until the next generation is in their 40s, 50s or even 60s.

Let's look at some other statistics that will become more relevant as we progress through this book:

- **Only 30% of Australian family businesses have established a succession plan.** This is concerning given the $3.5 trillion intergenerational wealth transfer expected over the next two decades.[1]
- **A high percentage of family businesses – around 77% – experienced growth in 2023, with 47% achieving double-digit increases in revenue.** This marks the highest growth rate in 15 years for this sector.[2]
- **Only 15% of Australia's family businesses report having robust digital capabilities.** However, nearly half are focusing on digital improvements to enhance competitiveness and resilience.[3]

---

1   KPMG, 'Family Offices Ignoring $3.5 Trillion Time Bomb', 2023, www.financialstandard.com.au/news/family-offices-ignoring-3-5tn-time-bomb-kpmg-179799855
2   PwC, 'Family Businesses See Largest Growth Increase in 15 Years: Traits Like Values, Employee Communication, Digital Capabilities Stand Out in Companies Which Outperformed Peers', 2023, www.pwc.com/gx/en/news-room/press-releases/2023/family-businesses-see-largest-growth-increase-in-15-years.html
3   PwC, 'Why Digital Transformation Should Be a Family (Business) Affair', 2021, www.pwc.com.au/digitalpulse/family-business-survey-digital-transformation.html

WELCOME

- **While 86% of Australian family businesses have some form of governance policy, only 27% have established a family constitution/charter.** This indicates a gap in formal governance structures that can impact succession planning and conflict resolution.[4]
- **Private and family businesses contribute approximately $600 billion to Australia's gross domestic product.** This demonstrates their substantial economic impact.[5]
- **Family-owned businesses are significant employers.** Family businesses employ approximately 50% of the Australian workforce.[6]
- **The average Australian family business has a turnover of $12 million and employs 37 people.** This highlights their substantial contribution to the economy.[7]
- **Only 8% of Australian family businesses have a robust succession plan.** This is well below the global average of 16%, reflecting a key vulnerability.[8]

---

4   PwC, 'Global Family Business Survey 2023: Australian Findings', 2023, www.pwc.com.au/pwc-private/family-business-survey.html; KPMG, 'Family Offices Ignoring $3.5 Trillion Time Bomb', 2023, www.financialstandard.com.au/news/family-offices-ignoring-3-5tn-time-bomb-kpmg-179799855
5   PwC, 'Once in a Lifetime: Australia's Intergenerational Succession', 2023, www.pwc.com.au/pwc-private/once-in-a-lifetime.html
6   Inside Small Business, 'Shining the Spotlight on Family Businesses', 2018, www.insidesmallbusiness.com.au/management/growth/shining-spotlight-on-family-businesses
7   Inside Small Business, 'Shining the Spotlight on Family Businesses', 2018, www.insidesmallbusiness.com.au/management/growth/shining-spotlight-on-family-businesses
8   CMA Australia, 'Family Businesses Optimistic but Future Growth at Risk', 2023, ontarget.cmaaustralia.edu.au/family-businesses-optimistic-but-future-growth-at-risk

- **Improving cash flow is the top challenge for family businesses.** In fact, 91% of Australian family businesses identify this as a primary concern.[9]
- **Only 15% of family businesses have a formal family employment policy.** This suggests governance practices are often informal, leaving room for improvement.[10]
- **Nearly 40% of Australian family businesses plan to sell or float.** Specifically, 38% are considering an exit strategy, compared to just 20% globally.[11]

Through these statistics, you can see how important family-owned businesses are to the Australian economy. Yet, they have a number of challenges to overcome, both as a group and as individual businesses.

There are definitely next-generation individuals who have wondered when their time to run the business would come.

A friend recalled to me the other day about a call they made to a local carpentry and cabinet company. They spoke with the owner, who was bright and cheerful and who delivered a high-quality display box for a client trade show. When the owner turned up, my friend was both delighted at the service and amazed at the owner, who turned out to be 91 and still living and working in the family timber yard. I enjoyed this little anecdote, as much for the passion of the owner as for the connection to my own family business, which operated in box making, packaging and timber for three generations.

---

9 Wybenga & Partners, 'Top 5 Challenges for Family Businesses', 2023, www.wybengapartners.com.au/2023/10/16/top-5-challenges-for-family-businesses
10 PwC, 'Global Family Business Survey 2023: Australian Findings', 2023, www.pwc.com.au/pwc-private/family-business-survey.html
11 CMA Australia, 'Family Businesses Optimistic but Future Growth at Risk', 2023, ontarget.cmaaustralia.edu.au/family-businesses-optimistic-but-future-growth-at-risk

Family farms running sheep, beef cattle or grain account for two out of three contributing family members across the entire agricultural sector.

One in 10 people working in a family business are in construction, with similarly high numbers in accommodation, food services and retail trade.

In short, family-run businesses matter to us, and they matter a lot.

They are a key pillar of the Australian economy.

Family business around the world

Australia is not alone. Around the world, small and family-owned businesses form the foundation of local economies. Yet despite their critical role, these businesses face many of the same challenges we've seen at home: succession planning is often delayed or overlooked, governance is frequently informal, and navigating digital transformation can be slow and uneven.

Understanding this global context gives us a broader perspective on the opportunities and risks facing family businesses today:

- **Family-owned businesses are global economic heavyweights.** They contribute over 70% of global GDP and employ around 60% of the global workforce.[12]
- **SMEs dominate the global business landscape.** They represent 90% of all businesses worldwide and are responsible for nearly 70% of employment.[13]

---

12 McKinsey & Company, 'All in the Family Business', 2023, www.mckinsey.com/featured-insights/sustainable-inclusive-growth/charts/all-in-the-family-business
13 World Economic Forum, 'Data Unleashed: Empowering SMEs for Innovation and Success', 2023, www3.weforum.org/docs/WEF_Data_Unleashed_Empowering_Small_and_Medium_Enterprises_(SMEs)_for_Innovation_and_Success_2023.pdf

- **The top 500 family businesses are a global force.** Together, they generate US$8.8 trillion in annual revenue – equivalent to the third-largest economy in the world.[14]
- **Growth has surged in recent years.** Approximately 43% of family businesses globally saw double-digit growth last financial year – the highest in 15 years.[15]
- **Formal family employment policies are rare.** Just 27% of family businesses globally have one in place, pointing to informal HR practices.[16]

These global figures paint a clear picture: family businesses are not just local engines of growth – they are pillars of the global economy. Yet with this prominence comes vulnerability. Without stronger governance, clearer succession plans, and greater adaptability to digital change, many of these enterprises risk falling short of their potential. As we continue exploring the dynamics of family business, it's vital to keep this broader context in mind – because the challenges we face here in Australia are part of a much larger, worldwide conversation.

The numbers are only the beginning

Yet the numbers are only the beginning of the discussion.

In many suburbs and communities around Australia, both urban and regional, there are family businesses that form a key part of the backbone of that community. It might be the local hardware store, a café, a fish and chip shop, or an accounting practice.

---

14 EY, '2025 EY and University of St.Gallen Global 500 Family Business Index', 2025, www.ey.com/en_gl/newsroom/2025/03/largest-500-family-businesses-amount-to-world-s-third-largest-economy
15 Wealth Briefing Asia, 'Family Businesses See Highest Growth in 15 Years', 2023, www.wealthbriefingasia.com/article.php?id=197364
16 PwC Australia, '11th Global Family Business Survey 2023', 2023, www.pwc.com.au/pwc-private/family-business-survey.html

Even though we've supposedly matured and grown as a country that operates on a global stage, the local family business is still a significant player in our minds, hearts and wallets. They are from *here*, not *there*. They are ours. A small, medium or even large business run by a family – sometimes for generations – loved and supported by locals, who consider it to be 'their own' and a part of the fabric of the suburb or community. They are supported because we know them, we know the family, we know the kids, and their business is one we need in our community for our daily bread, our fish and chips, our house maintenance.

Even in this 21st century, the family running the cake shop, the café, the local computer service team or the local builder are known and supported by their customers and locals – because of their products and services, but also for who they are.

You only have to think for a moment about businesses we all know that trade on their family origins:

- Bundaberg Rum
- Haigh's Chocolates
- Brown Brothers
- De Bortoli Wines
- Linfox
- Harris Farm Markets.

And I'm sure many more who are lesser known on a national scale, but very well known by the communities they serve.

Some of the family-owned businesses that I've worked for include Quickmail, Belpile, Dracula's, Filter Supplies, Dorsett Retail and Coogee Chemicals.

Speaking to colleagues in the consulting industry and other friends of mine, I've heard of successful fourth-generation family businesses building homes – Hibbard Homes, based in Coffs Harbour, NSW – others making yoghurt, still others delivering much-needed first aid training, and all shapes, manners, sizes and styles of business that you could imagine.

Your business is one of those.

Since you are in the family business, you contribute an important part of this overall impact of family-owned business. Maybe that contribution is not as important to you as simply earning enough to put the kids through school, pay off the mortgage and have a holiday or two a year, but the contribution is meaningful nonetheless.

Australia is one of the few countries that seeks to measure and record the impact of family-owned businesses. They are recognised as important.

This doesn't mean that the government necessarily goes out of its way to support family businesses. Even though the value is recognised, there isn't some out-of-the-box, out-of-the-ordinary support for families who run businesses. They still have to deal with government red tape, legislation and tax like any other business.

Despite their value to the economy, the community, the suburb, and to the family itself, families are not perfect at running their own businesses. If they were, there would be no need for a book like this.

Families running businesses are at the mercy of similar issues as every other business.

Often, they are in business because the founder had a passion for growing grapes, delivering goods, making coffee or growing wheat. They are not in business because they loved the idea of business itself; it is more likely a product or service passion or a technical skill.

That brings me to the observation that there were very few places in the past where you could learn how to operate a business, let alone a family business. Even today, there are very few institutions that offer education in family business.

What this means is the learning environment has mostly been on the job. This is true for the founder, and it remains true for the next and subsequent generations.

Sons and daughters learn from mothers and fathers. They learn from their uncles and aunts, as well as older cousins. Sometimes this means the next generation can inherit poor business management from their parents. Sometimes it means the older generation continues to insist that business is done their way, even when they've supposedly handed over the reins to the kids.

In short, families running businesses run into all the challenges and issues of businesses in general. They can also deal with problems unique to family business, such as nepotism and patronage, such as who gets to own shares, and what is fair and what is equal when businesses are transitioned to a new generation.

Are fair and equal the same thing?

No, they are not, or at least not necessarily.

With family, you get the whole range of human behaviours, abilities, opinions, egos and skills, all wrapped up in a group of individuals to whom you are tied by blood, no matter what business role you play.

Families can suffer from members who work hard and get less than they would in an alternative corporate setting. They can suffer from family members who want more than they are due in relation to their work, or their shareholding, or both.

Some can try to take advantage because it's a family business. Some may steal from family members.

This can mean family business can be uniquely sticky to navigate sometimes.

You have a place in your family: first born, the smart one, the quiet one, the fiery one, the risk taker, the black sheep.

And you have a role in the business.

These two things are not the same.

Yet they are intertwined inevitably and must be navigated for your family and your family business to survive.

Progress not perfection

Some years ago I was invited into a business run by an inventor and some investor shareholders.

The inventor was a genius and had worked out a natural way to handle a major problem at many levels of society – in healthcare, in travel and in agriculture. He had 'almost' finished dozens of different applications at all different scales of this product. Small to large, one person to thousands.

It was incredibly simple yet powerful technology.

When the business invited me in, they were bleeding cash and about to close. I asked if there were any product applications we could commercialise immediately to get some cash moving.

The investors showed me one product ready to go that we could sell.

I asked them how long it would take to produce 1000 units.

Well, you wouldn't have seen more smoke from the screeching of brakes in a road train.

'It isn't ready!' said the inventor.

'But it works,' I replied.

'It's not perfect,' he answered.

'Let's make it version 1.0,' I suggested. 'Then, when you make some improvements, we'll launch a new version, and another and another. At least we'll get moving and you'll have some cash to pay the bills.'

The inventor, unfortunately, couldn't let go of the idea of perfection, would not change his mind, and the business folded.

This will be a recurring theme in this book.

I'll share some tools and stories and guide you on your journey. But it won't be perfect.

Your family may still have disagreements. You won't see eye to eye on every business idea. Progress not perfection should be your catchcry.

If you can move forward, improve, tinker, and realise it is an ongoing journey of discovery and outcomes, you'll do okay.

Don't be like the inventor. Be willing to accept progress, no matter how small a step forward; it is still going to be in the right direction, or a new direction not previously considered.

My life in family business

As a young boy, I'd visit one of the sites in our family's diversified business with my father. At the time, it was run by my grandfather and located out on Geelong Road in Brooklyn. It felt like a long trip from Kew, winding through Footscray before the Westgate Bridge existed.

Poppa, as everyone called him, would drive me around in his little three-wheeled electric buggy through giant, noisy sheds. I'd chat with the workers, marvel at the machines, and rummage through the stationery cupboard in the office like it was my own personal Officeworks.

Poppa was deeply respected – by staff, suppliers and family alike. Years later, at a truck stop in remote Eucla, a stranger saw my surname on a bank card and asked, 'Are you related to Poppa Broons?' He then shared stories about how admired Poppa was. In the middle of nowhere, his legacy still resonated.

Our business began with wooden fruit boxes, expanded into timber merchandising and milling, and eventually moved into construction, even owning a Ford dealership. When wooden boxes gave way to cardboard, we adapted, pivoting into corrugated packaging.

In 1970, our family business was sold, though Dad kept parts of it going. When I was 17, I started working in operations – stacking timber, making up orders, and eventually getting a beat-up Ford Falcon company ute as my first car. I worked across different areas – from sawmills to prefab framing – and learned the business from the ground up. Once, fresh with my licence, I was tasked with setting out a construction site with no clue where to start. Thankfully, a couple of kind carpenters helped me apply my high-school geometry in the real world.

Later, I worked overseas in the US with a family-run business – albeit one with 68,000 employees and its own forests around Mount St Helens. That time taught me a lot, including how events like the eruption of Mount St Helens could shift a company's strategy – and why adaptability matters.

On returning, I brought back ideas, but as my father was in charge, I learned an important lesson: change doesn't happen just because you have good ideas. It takes buy-in.

Dad passed away in 1983, just before I had the chance to work closely beside him as planned. My sister, who had long worked at his side, stepped in. Later, in 1991, I negotiated to buy the business from the family.

Down the track, I was involved with setting up Family Business Australia, which is now the Family Business Association.

My lifelong interest in people – fostered in those early days around the office, the factory floor, and with my clients – still shapes how I approach family businesses today.

Generational transitions

We are born, we grow, we mature, we decline, we die.

This is an eternal truth of the life of one human. But it is not the lifecycle of a species, nor a civilisation. These things last over much longer timescales.

In all species, there is procreation, and in all species the parents play a role in the early survival and education of their offspring. The human family is no different, and while the concept of the nuclear family may be changing in our 21st-century society, there is still support, nurturing and wisdom passed from parents to children.

We all want our kids to grow up, be healthy, be financially secure, and have opportunities to repeat the pattern with their own families.

For financial security, some of us choose to own and operate a business to pay the bills, buy food and shelter, and fund the next generation's education and passage into adulthood.

Sometimes these businesses survive beyond the founder and become a source of financial security and prosperity for not only the next generation but also a growing number of descendant family members.

Generation to generation, getting married, having kids, and then seeing them get married and have kids can exponentially grow the number of family members involved in the family business.

What started out with a 'simple' purpose of financial security for one family can quickly escalate into hundreds, if not thousands, of relations involved as owners, operators and/or dependents.

Complexity?

Sure!

Impossibility?

Definitely not!

This book is about the transition.

But it isn't *only* about the transition.

Transitions can be complicated.

There are considerations of family, considerations of ownership, and considerations of the actual running of the business.

You can roll headlong into transition, and you'll probably run into issues.

I've seen many of these issues arise.

Sometimes they are solved. Sometimes they absolutely break families and destroy businesses.

I'm not your typical business consultant. I focus on the family first. A strong, aligned family can use the business as a tool to achieve their goals. In my view, you can't fix a family by fixing a business – but help the family, and they can fix the business.

Think of the business as a hammer. If someone drives a nail in sideways, you don't blame the hammer – you help the person using it. That's how I work.

If you want a successful transition, start with your family. A well-functioning family can run a successful business.

Why we come together

Sometimes we might think we're better off alone.

But no one can survive for long on their own.

Even with significant scientific advancements, the chances of one individual or one species achieving immortality are currently considered extremely unlikely.

But there is one way we can achieve some measure of immortality, and that is through our children and their children's children.

The basic group or unit through which this occurs is the family.

Why do we come together with other humans?

Well, the answer is as old as civilisation.

Through recorded history, we've been gathering in larger and larger groups to promote better survival for ourselves, our families and our groups.

Someone is always going to be better at hunting, someone at gathering.

Today, someone will be better at numbers, and someone else better with people.

Groups come together and eventually disband on the basis of shared goals – survival, growth, protection, food, shelter, services – you name it; we have to have something that is shared for us to come together.

It is the basis of social groups, and indeed clans, tribes, cultures and organisations.

Sometimes, the shared purpose is a want, not a need – such as a group of mates who enjoy the same sport or pastimes.

But something is shared. Something is aligned.

It is to these shared 'things' that I attend to first when I work with families who own businesses.

If you're hit by a bus

Family businesses can be difficult, simply because you've added another dimension of FAMILY into BUSINESS.

On being organised and planning for the challenges you'll face, I wrote a book some time ago called *If You're Hit by a Bus: 27 questions most people in business can't answer*. I've republished this in the appendix of this book.

It is wise to ask these questions with your family. Working through the answers together as a family makes a huge difference. Maybe even having a trusted person on hand who understands the family can be a big help in supporting each family member through these discussions.

Sometimes, bringing in an independent adviser – someone the family trusts, but who isn't part of the day-to-day – can make it easier to have open conversations. It can help surface different views, challenge assumptions and reduce the impact of biases or old family dynamics. A good adviser doesn't take over – they simply guide the process so everyone has the space to be heard, and so the family can make strong, clear decisions together.

STEP 1

STEP 1

UNITE

the key to creating a thriving enterprise

'United we stand, divided we fall.'
Aesop, *The Bundle of Sticks*

If a family can't work together, the family business is at risk of having more than one agenda driving it, which can damage relationships with suppliers, customers, or those employed within the business.

In a family business, unity is the key to creating a thriving enterprise.

Having a united family doesn't mean there won't be stormy periods within the business or the family. The dynamics of a family are constantly changing, from new partners entering and exiting to the entry of the next generation, and more.

Each change shifts the dynamic of the family and the business, sometimes just a little and sometimes a lot.

When I begin working with a family preparing for a generational transition, my first step is to understand each individual. I speak one-on-one with every family member who owns or works in the business – and often with partners or children, even if they're not involved day to day.

Why? Because I'm looking for insight into their perspectives, concerns, roles, and relationships. In many family businesses, unspoken assumptions drive decisions. When these stay beneath the surface, they can create tension and block effective communication.

My role is to surface both the positives and the challenges in a constructive way. Sometimes, parents have promised the business to their children, but progress is slow – too slow for the next generation. In other cases, the older generation holds on tight to control, or siblings are pitted against each other. The famous feud between the Dassler brothers, which split the family and gave rise to Adidas and Puma, is a powerful reminder of what's at stake.

My goal is always unity – but not at the expense of the individual. I want each family member to pursue their own path while also exploring how those paths might align to achieve shared aspirations.

Is it possible? Absolutely.

Is it easy? Not always.

Understanding your business

Over my years working with families in business, I have found that those who can unite behind a single purpose or goal are able to manage thriving businesses, regardless of the challenges or storms they face.

The first stage in any successful family business is finding out where you are all aligned and what your values are. When I talk about values, I mean guiding principles for your life and business.

Values act as a decision-making anchor. When tensions arise – and they will – shared values give you something to return to, something stable that overcomes individual opinions or short-term pressures. They will not work if they are vague aspirations you write down once and forget. They need to be real, lived, and visible in the way the family communicates, governs, and makes decisions.

> Misalignment on values is one of the most common causes of conflict in family businesses.

It can show up subtly, like disagreements over growth strategy, or more overtly, like clashes about leadership roles or succession. But when families take the time to articulate and agree on what truly matters to them, they create a foundation that supports not just commercial success, but harmony and longevity.

You also have to be clear on who owns the business and how it is owned. For example, is it a partnership, a trust, or a privately held company with shareholders? The structure matters because it should reflect – and support – the family's shared values, particularly around control, responsibility, and fairness.

I've come across families over the years who do talk about their values and what they believe. They might be operating from spiritual values, such as those of Christianity or Judaism, or they might be some other set of values. Some even write them down.

There is a wonderfully extreme example of this in a family from Japan who have written family values that have stayed the same in their business for over 400 years. They are the Mogi family – and while you may have never heard their name, you know their product: Kikkoman Soy Sauce.

'Isogaba maware' is a Japanese axiom that translates into 'make haste slowly'.

A rough translation means that you should advance and grow, but do so with tremendous thought and care. Kikkoman has exemplified this philosophy since its humble beginnings in the 17th century. This was a time when power in Japan was not with the emperor but with the Shogun or military leaders. Land ownership and military service were intertwined, and it was during this period that the Mogi first perfected a meticulous six-month brewing process to make Kikkoman Soy Sauce.

A family business to this day, the generational success of Kikkoman has been inspired by a family creed comprising 16 guiding statements passed down for not just one or two generations but an incredible 19. This creed speaks to the core values that have enabled Kikkoman to survive and thrive for more than 400 years. Here it is, translated from Japanese.

My counsel to you is to take the time to sit down with your family and communicate. Through this communication of your individual needs and wants, and your shared goals, you will be able to create a statement of shared values and a purpose for your business that could still be operating hundreds of years from now.

What a legacy that would be!

KIKKOMAN'S MOGI FAMILY CREED

Article I. All family members desire peace. Never fight, and always respect each other. Ensure progress in business and the perpetuation of family prosperity.

Article II. Loving God and Buddha is the source of all virtue. Keeping faith leads to a peaceful mind.

Article III. All family members should be polite to each other. If the master is not polite, the others will not follow. Sin is the result of being impolite. Families – young and old, masters and workers – govern themselves by politeness; then peace will be brought of their own accord.

Article IV. Virtue is the cause, fortune the effect. Never mistake the cause for the effect. Never judge people on whether they are rich or not.

Article V. Keep strict discipline. Demand diligence. Preserve order – young and old, master and workers.

Article VI. Business depends on people. Do not make appointments or dismissals using personal prejudices. Put the right man in the right place. Loving men who do what they should bring peace to their minds.

Article VII. Education of the children is our responsibility to the nation. Train the body and mind with moral, intellectual and physical education.

Article VIII. Approach all living beings with love. Love is fundamental to human beings and the source of a life worth living. Words are the door to fortune and misfortune. A foul tongue hurts oneself and others. A kind tongue keeps everything peaceful. Be careful in every word you speak.

Article IX. Keep humbleness and diligence, which have been handed down over the years from our forefathers. Make every effort to do as much as you can.

Article X. True earning comes from the labour of sweat. Speculation is not the best road to follow. Don't do business by taking advantage of another's weakness.

Article XI. Competition is an important factor in progress, but avoid extreme or unreasonable competition. Strive to prosper together with the public.

Article XII. Make success or failure clear, judge fairly punishment and reward. Never fail to reward meritorious service, and don't allow a mistake to go unpunished.

Article XIII. Consult with family members when starting a new business. Never try to do anything alone. Always appreciate any profit made by your family.

Article XIV. Don't carelessly fall into debt. Don't recklessly be a guarantor of liability. Don't lend money with the purpose of gaining interest, because you are not a bank.

Article XV. Save money from your earnings and give to society as much as you can. But never ask for a reward nor think highly of yourself.

Article XVI. Don't decide important affairs by yourself. Always consult with the people concerned before making a decision. Then employees will have a positive attitude in their work.

Understanding yourself

If you're reading this book, you may be in your mid-20s to mid-40s. You probably have an idea of who you are. You will know how you learn, your own level of self-esteem, and you will have a sense of your place in the world.

In the context of your family business, knowing who you are is important because you will be involved with other people in trying to make the business work. Knowing yourself helps you in the process of dealing with other people and the way they work.

In a family, we always carry a label – Mum is always Mum, Dad is always Dad, number one child, number two child. You might be the funny one, the hard worker, or the smart one.

You've possibly carried this label throughout your life. It's important to know who you are because once you step through the door of the business to work, that label should fall away as you take on a title, role or position within the business.

Your family label is not your business role.

Now you're in your family's business, I want to ask you a few questions.

I ask a lot of questions, as you'll find in this book.

- Do you like being in the business?
- How much training have you had in this job?
- Are you coming in having experienced work and life outside of the family business?

Once you know who you are and you've decided you *do* want to stay in the business, the next questions are:

- Where do you want to go within the business?

- Have you thought about your capabilities and what else you need to know?
- What other learnings might you need to take on the top job, or is that even your desire?
- How well do you know the plans that other family members have for their future?

You need to start asking yourself what more you need to know or understand about the business your family is in that you don't already know.

It starts with unity

I grew up around family businesses, often interacting with friends and contacts – including high-net-worth individuals – who were part of them. Even casual conversations offered lessons; much of what I learned came from simply soaking in the experience, often unintentionally.

Today I regularly speak with members across multiple family generations. One trusted confidante, who had listened to me talk at length about my work, once said, 'You actually have quite a formal approach and model for how you work with families.'

She was right. While my method is instinctive and shaped by experience, it follows a clear, step-by-step process to guide clients toward success.

What I'm sharing in this book is deeply personal. I didn't sketch a model and then test it – it evolved the other way around. Lived experience led to process, which led to conversation, which became a codified model.

It all starts with UNITE.

When I experienced families who were arguing or divided over the family business, I saw there was a need for them to UNITE as a family before anything more positive could be achieved in that business. I could see they needed to identify a purpose for what they were doing and also codify a set of values for how they wanted to operate as a family.

This was intuitive, and over the years I've found a way to help them do that. I believe that there is no point in me 'telling' them what those values should be, nor dictating a purpose or goal for them and their business.

It has to come from the family, and as such, my way of advising is to ask a lot of questions, listen a lot, and then guide my clients towards creating these things for themselves, in their own words. Only then will the purpose and values be meaningful to them as a group and as individual family members within that group.

Of course, before anyone can UNITE, they need to know this is important.

From unknowing to knowing

Within the UNITE stage, the first journey each family member takes is from unknowing to knowing. This results in:

- clarity of their own personal identity
- clarity of the family
- clarity of the business.

Once each member of the family has clarity, they're able to make better choices, and to really *understand* why they are making those choices. They are not just random or reflexive actions based on unknown or unclear facts and information.

The UNITE step is about understanding that if we're a family and if we're in business, we need to understand each other, what we're doing, why we are doing it, and how we work together as a family. This takes honesty and communication, and sometimes it can cause ripples or even tsunamis, but the honesty, communication and understanding are essential to achieve a great outcome for the family and therefore the family business.

Each of us grows up with our own way of seeing the world: there are things we're aware of and things we're not.[17] As each individual in the family travels their own life journey, all of the life incidents that happen to one person help shape that person. We can never know about every life experience of another person, and even if we did, we would still be forced to look at it from our point of view, which will give us a different perspective; our truth will be slightly different from theirs.

It takes time and effort to learn and understand our family, our business and other businesses, and gain the tools to manage it all. As businesses grow, more people join the company, bringing with them expertise and knowledge that may or may not have previously existed in the business but are necessary for continued growth. The more people, the more complexity and opportunity for challenge, and the greater the necessity for understanding the family and the business.

> As individuals, we should always be striving to learn as much as we can and to be sufficiently transparent so that others in the family and the business can thrive.

---

17 This relates to a concept called the Johari Window. The Johari Window is a model for understanding self-awareness and interpersonal communication. It describes four areas of knowledge: what is known or unknown to ourselves and to others.

Each family member needs to make a choice whether or not to grow, to expand their universe. It is perfectly okay if you don't want to grow or don't want to grow within the family business.

Why does the business exist?

A family exists to create a stable environment for the next generation of kids to grow up, learn things, and be set up so they can survive and look after themselves, because we're not going to be around forever.

A family business can be an extension or a vehicle for the current generation to support that objective for the family by creating a place where the kids can work, learn the ropes and then take over, supporting their financial security for as long as they need, and maybe to repeat the process in 20 or 30 years for their kids.

But a business is a commercial entity – it exists for profit. The bigger a business gets, the more potential owners or shareholders it has, and the more people it has who are reliant on those profits being made.

This is not the same objective as that of a family. Yet the two entities of family and business – and their respective goals – can co-exist if you are willing to take the steps necessary to craft this symbiotic relationship when it comes to a family-run enterprise.

Defining family and business roles

A large challenge comes with confusing the two entities, confusing the 'hat' each family member wears in each entity, and how the two can be connected successfully. The family and the business may be joined at the hip, but they are functionally separate things.

An individual's role in the family is not replaceable. But what if you have to sack an underperforming family member from the business? You'd better have some agreements and processes in place to handle that! That person is probably going to take it personally.

But how many times have you heard *business is not personal* – and it is true.

Family is personal.

Business is for profit.

Is it any wonder the UNITE step is so important?

Sitting around a dinner table is the way many businesses become family businesses. It's those conversations that your parents bring home because they are too busy during the working day or they are asked to share highlights and changes happening in the business.

These conversations connect you emotionally even though you may not have even set foot on the premises. Over time, the business grows, and opportunities become available for you to spend time after school, on weekends or on holidays at the family business.

This is a really special time, where we are learning our business. We learn, we talk, and we grow in our understanding of how our family makes things work.

During this time, we also have moments when we disagree or argue. In most cases, we get positive outcomes and we learn about our family dynamic. This is where we are set up to become a true family in business.

It is also a place where we learn more about each family member and how we interact with our business systems and each other.

So long as we keep coming together and we are honest with each other about our reasoning and our feelings, we can move on together with a common aim of growing the family business.

We have our natural leader, the entrepreneur who started this business. All of us who follow will generally have bought into the leader's vision.

The younger family members are interested and learning something new. Those a bit older already know how things are done but not necessarily how finance is managed or processes are created. And then there are those who have been working in the business for some time and can see different ways of doing things but don't have any say in how things are done.

When complexity arises

It's quite a surprise when you first find out that your point of view isn't necessarily the way things work. In a business sense, it likely happens when you start doing something you've been instructed to do and someone else comes along to tell you that's not how this should be done.

In smaller businesses, generally, many of the processes and procedures are not written down and we have to make our own decisions about how we do things to get the job done. There may be little supervision and little instruction when you begin.

The larger the business and the more complicated the work, hopefully there will be more instruction and guidance, but that still leaves opportunity for an individual either not to follow the rules or to change parts of the rules as they work through the job.

Everybody sees much of what is done through their own perspective. It's not intentional that we see things differently. It's the fact that each of us has travelled our own journey and our life experience has given us this view of the world.

This is when open conversations are required. Open conversations are about communicating your thoughts and ideas honestly, so that the others in the conversation have a true understanding of your thoughts and feelings, so long as each person in the conversation is being true to their values.

Values are reflected in how and why each individual makes decisions.

Open conversations allow us to reveal and address inconsistencies in thinking, and should enable us to avoid conflict through understanding different perspectives.

Another complexity can be a family member defying expectations and choosing not to work in the business. Each family member needs to respect that every other family member has their own journey to travel. Sometimes family members will work outside of the business and come back many years later. Sometimes people don't have the required skill set, and sometimes family members just don't get along.

Whatever the reason, it should be recognised that it is okay for an individual, once they are over 18, to make their own choices. As much as parents want the best for their children and they have strong ideas of what that entails, it may be better in the long run to let the younger generation find their own path.

We need to think of a family as its own ecosystem and therefore, like a business, it needs a solid foundation. Family values create a solid foundation, and will help you navigate the inevitable complexities. They become guideposts that all of the family congregate around in tough times; some families in business reference their values as their north stars. They provide a definition of how we, as a family, behave and most importantly what we collectively value. As our guideposts, they help with our decision-making, guiding an individual family member (or a collection of family members) back to what truly matters to us as a family. It makes choices easier.

But as a family, we need to recognise that the addition of new family members may bring a new set of values. We therefore need to acknowledge that the values aren't set in stone; they can shift and change as time progresses.

What is important is that the family remains on the same page about them, and if there is a deviation from them, the family is gently guided back to these principles.

I have spent my life being true to my family values, and while they have shifted and changed over the years, many of them have remained the same. Values such as family, honesty and trust have always been the cornerstones of my family's values and are carried on via my own children even today.

The importance of good communication

After you and your family have sat down together to map out shared values, what does the UNITE step entail?

I want each individual to succeed and prosper, and I think we should always ensure we aren't sacrificing one for the many when, with choice, both the one and the many can win.

To help with this, I use a Genogram. Without getting into a nitty-gritty explanation, it is a tool that functions as a detailed family tree that maps out relationships, key dynamics and historical patterns within the family. The Genogram serves as a visual aid to identify areas of conflict and alliance, and potential areas of concern.

By leveraging this tool, I am able to help family members pinpoint key relationship dynamics and facilitate discussions that might otherwise be difficult to initiate.

Inevitably, we are 'talking about talking' here. Communication.

Sometimes, the first person these individual family members talk to is me.

For the first time, they really share their goals and aspirations. They share the things they love about their family and the members they get on with. They share the issues, challenges, concerns and upsets, and perhaps members of the family that they do not get on with. Sometimes they share their view on tense relationships between one of their siblings and a parent.

Either way, I'm not digging for dirt. I'm digging for opportunity.

These conversations can be incredibly difficult to have with a parent, a child or a sibling – which is why having a neutral, paid external adviser is often essential. My role is to create a safe space where honesty is possible, and where difficult truths can be aired without fear of damaging relationships.

In my mind, conflict or disagreement is an opportunity. An opportunity for a third solution. A lack of transparency can create resentment and confusion, ultimately leading to tensions that impact both the family and the business itself.

Imagine there is a number written on a pavement between you and another person.

You look down and see the number 6.

The other person – maybe your dad – looks down and sees a number 9.

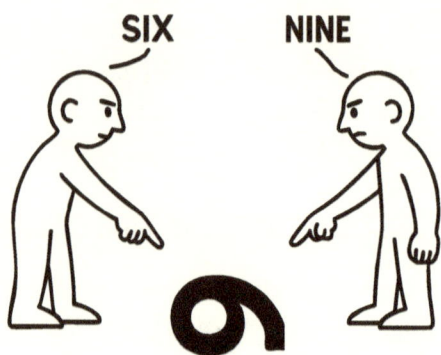

You argue and argue your point, insisting on your rightness.

Yet the thing is, you are *both* right – from your viewpoint.

Viewpoint is an interesting thing.

Two people witnessing an accident from different locations will describe two different scenarios – these might agree or they might not. The fact is, it is impossible for two people to share the exact same viewpoint on something. Our viewpoints are a function of not only our location but also our upbringing, education, life experience and skill sets.

One person might see a situation as a huge challenge.

Another may overcome it easily.

> You don't have to share the exact same viewpoint to agree on a shared course of action.

But you do have to take the time to share the individual viewpoints – the good, bad and ugly – to form an open communication environment in which to find shared agreements.

Agreements and shared values cannot exist where ideas, needs, wants, aspirations and expectations are not communicated or shared. This is the purpose of my one-on-one conversations and the Genogram.

There was one family I worked with where deep-seated misunderstandings and unaddressed grievances had created significant barriers to progress. Through structured dialogue and trust-building exercises, I was able to help them navigate these challenges and foster a more open and collaborative approach to decision-making.

A journey towards shared values

There is complexity in family businesses, particularly when we start focusing on values, communication and purpose.

What people perceive externally about a family is only a fraction of what truly exists within. Much like when you observe a neighbour in their garden, you have no idea of what happens inside their home.

Similarly, the internal workings of a family business are deeply rooted in values that may not always be visible. These values influence how individuals act and react, sometimes causing internal conflicts when unspoken or misaligned.

By fostering a culture of transparency, trust and proactive planning, family businesses can achieve greater long-term success. Once everything is on the metaphorical 'table', we can gather around a physical table to work towards shared values.

I encourage you, as a family member who is about to hand over the reins of a business or take the reins from a parent or relative, to take the time to have individual discussions with your family members. Then create an environment where you can establish your shared values.

This could be a retreat where you and the other family members take time out of the business as a family to meet. It could be simply a few hours around the boardroom table to talk values.

In concise terms, here are some steps a family could take to become more united:

1. Invite all the family stakeholders to a 'values' workshop.
2. At the meeting, start by sharing what you've learned from individual discussions.
3. Make sure you keep these productive and forward-looking, focusing on solutions rather than negativity and conflict.
4. Invite individuals to share their ideas on values and put these simply on a whiteboard or butcher's paper.
5. Once each person has shared ideas – ensuring contributions from everyone – have some sort of voting process where people choose their top three, four or five values.
6. Tally up the votes and open the floor for discussion on these shared and voted-for values.
7. Is there general agreement that these are the shared values?
8. Write some words – maybe a sentence or a paragraph on each – to explain and expand on the value or word and what it means to the family.[18]

---

[18] In reality, it usually takes an external viewpoint to achieve the best outcomes from exercises like this. In my experience, families who try to do these things on their own never fully resolve issues. If one family member acts as a facilitator, they bring their own viewpoints and vested interests. So having a family adviser – such as the role I play for families I work with – is a smart choice if you want to get the most out of these discussions and actions.

Here are six value examples from the Mogi Family Creed that I mentioned earlier:

1. **Family:** Ensure progress and family prosperity.
2. **People:** Business depends on people.
3. **Diligence:** Make every effort to do as much as you can.
4. **Clarity:** Clearly communicate success or failure.
5. **Prudence:** Don't carelessly fall into debt.
6. **Give:** Give to society as much as you can.

Individuals can behave in ways that do not align with their values or fit into social or familial expectations. This creates internal pressure, manifesting as discomfort or a 'gut feeling' that things are amiss for all concerned.

> It is so important to take the time to identify and articulate values within a family business to ensure coherence and alignment among its members.

Open communication plays a crucial role in this process, as your family must establish ways to discuss and reinforce shared values.

I'll share a relevant experience with a family-run prosthetics manufacturing business. While the business was initially operating harmoniously, it started to experience internal discord as it expanded. Through a values workshop, I worked with them to identify core business values by compiling individual staff inputs on a whiteboard.

A notable revelation was the word 'timeliness', which one staff member felt strongly about but which had no support from other employees. This was ultimately dismissed by the business owners.

The employee who championed it later chose to leave the company, having realised her values did not align with the organisation's culture. Even though she wasn't a family member, the learning from this situation holds true when dealing with family members who have different approaches or values.

Once the individual left the business, the harmonious workplace environment returned.

This example highlights how significant the alignment of values is in ensuring workplace harmony and potential success. Those in your family business must recognise the things they agree on and their differences, and then make conscious choices about their involvement in the business.

The above exercise is a structured process that will help you transition from an unconscious understanding of your business's values to a clearly articulated framework. This self-awareness enables better decision-making, particularly concerning hiring family members.

Families may employ relatives out of convenience, obligation or tradition. Understanding values ensures these decisions are made with clarity and intention.

Cultural and historical backgrounds also influence family dynamics and business operations. Different cultural upbringings can influence ideas and decision-making about finances. For instance, a person raised in a low-income household may have a vastly different approach to money compared to someone from a wealthy household. These differences must be acknowledged and managed to avoid conflicts.

A journey towards shared purpose

Shared value statements are important. Equally important are business purpose statements. Why are we running this business? How does it intersect with our family values? What are our lifestyle priorities? What are our motivations?

Purpose statements can range from a concise paragraph to an extensive document, but whatever form they take, they must resonate deeply with all family members involved.

> Establishing a clear purpose aids in decision-making and provides direction for the business's future.

The purpose statement can form the foundation of a family charter, a formalised document outlining the business's principles, values and governance structure.

I worked with a family that had a historical coat of arms featuring a dagger holding a snowball, symbolising an ancestral obligation to present a snowball to the king. Integrating such historical elements into the family charter can reinforce the family legacy and values.

As families define their purpose, they must also address roles within the business.

In families, we have familial roles. In business, we have professional roles.

Workplace responsibilities probably should not be – but often are – influenced by birth order or childhood labels. Separating the two roles is important. In the case of business roles, they should be clearly defined, with job descriptions, responsibilities and expectations.

Family members should be held accountable for their contributions to the business. Having a written charter ensures that expectations are explicit, reducing ambiguity and potential disputes. If individual family members fail to meet expectations, the family has predetermined and agreed approaches that can be implemented fairly instead of reactively.

Imagine you had family members who, due to some physical or mental challenge, were not able to contribute to the business equally. In this case, the family might decide that it has a role to support that individual through their life, and the otherwise skill- or role-based agreements are adapted for that circumstance. It becomes a recognised, agreed and fairly implemented system.

A friend shared an example with me the other day of a café owner he knows who has a child with Down syndrome. This child has limitations, but within a certain role, performs very well. Maybe he can't take on complex sales negotiations, but his help in the kitchen with food preparation is excellent and welcomed by both the family and the customers of that café.

Or family businesses may decide that the business plays a role in setting aside funds for education for the next generation. University costs may be paid in exchange for the enhanced skill set then being deployed in the business for a few years.

This diagram outlines the differing priorities of three key family business stakeholders: the retiring parent, the active successor, and family members not employed in the business. Each has distinct concerns – from retirement security and harmony (retiring parent), to authority and growth capital (successor), to fairness and investment returns (non-employed members). Achieving alignment between these diverse needs requires a unified family vision and a clear business strategy. When successfully integrated, these lead to a shared future vision for the family business, balancing legacy, leadership and long-term sustainability.

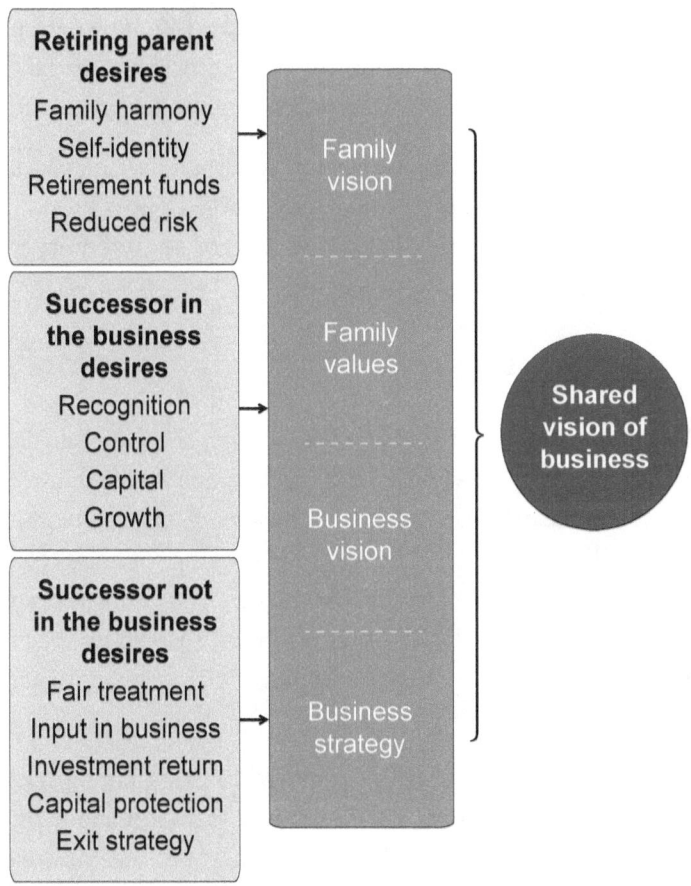

Capturing and transferring wisdom

Family businesses can balance history and individual contributions while maintaining clear communication and shared values and purpose. By understanding and documenting their purpose and values, families can create businesses that are both successful and harmonious.

In many businesses, this means that the leaders need to recognise the importance of documenting and passing down their knowledge. I've observed that many experienced business owners and executives operate with a wealth of tacit knowledge but fail to formally capture and transfer this wisdom to the next generation.

This lack of documentation can create significant obstacles during succession planning and executive transitions. There is a need for structured knowledge-sharing processes to ensure continuity and stability within businesses.

Time to UNITE

Many of the challenges faced by family enterprises are mirrored in corporate settings, where unclear succession plans and ineffective communication can lead to disruptions. When I'm working with families on this UNITE step, I'm looking for an outcome where the family is in a position to make better decisions because they know more about each other, and they understand the reasons they are better off together, operating from shared values and purpose.

You should find, as you do the work of collating family values and have more conversations with family members about their individual needs, wants and desires, that you'll reach a point where your purpose as a family is clear, and where that interacts with a business, that the purpose of the business is also clearer to you as a family.

Inevitably, models are a simplification or division of real life. They are meant to make it easier to do a series of small steps that add up to a much bigger result. I would advise you not to slavishly follow these steps in a sequential order and think it is a one-time deal. In real life, I've started at different points in this model depending on where the family was at. I've also returned to do further work in a step of the model when circumstances change.

Yes, it is useful to have all the actions and documented values and purpose to achieve the outcomes of each step. Yet, you can also survive and thrive by making sure they are done even if they are not done in order. You can always adjust your ideas, values, business purpose, roles, strategy and anything else you want if circumstances or situations change over time.

The Mogi family may have upheld the same core creed for 19 generations, but even they would have adapted how they lived out that creed in the context of their times. The soy sauce recipe might remain unchanged, but their charitable giving, for example, likely looks very different today than it did in 1683.

> Be flexible, understand each step of the model and the tools that will help you and your family thrive, and put in the work.

If you're willing to invest the time and energy, I can (almost) guarantee the process and the outcomes will be better for it.

I'd like to conclude this chapter with a brief activity that you can use to benchmark yourself and your family in terms of shared values and family closeness.

Exercise: Reflecting on UNITE

If you've successfully completed the UNITE step, you should have:

- clearly articulated family values
- a shared understanding of why you're better together
- a sense of what the family wants to achieve
- clarity around the purpose of the family business.

Take a few minutes now to consolidate that clarity.

1. In your own words, write down the purpose of your family business:

   ....
   ....
   ....
   ....

2. List your top three shared family values:

   ....
   ....
   ....

3. Describe one way your family is stronger together than apart:

   ....
   ....
   ....
   ....
   ....

4. What is one shared goal the family wants to achieve in the next five years?

   ....
   ....
   ....
   ....
   ....

5. Reflect: What did you personally learn or realise during the UNITE step?

   ....
   ....
   ....
   ....
   ....

STEP 2

STEP 2

BUILD
align your family with the business

'You can go faster alone but farther together.'
African proverb

The Build stage is really all about having the family understand the difference between being an employee, and having a business and working on growing a business while learning the business itself.

A business that is going to transition from one generation to another has probably been in operation for some time. The next generation coming in may have worked elsewhere and gained some skills they are bringing into the business. Or they might have only worked in the family business, in various roles from part-time work after school to helping in operations, admin or sales.

The current generation are the leaders of the business, and need to help the next generation learn how to lead, not just perform technical or specialist functions, but be able to run it.

Sometimes there is a lack of transparency, and the younger generation can't answer the question: is there a place for me in this business moving forward? Sometimes parents promise things, but then when push comes to shove, they are not ready to hand over the reins at a time when the younger generation is getting 'ants in their pants' and wants to take over or start taking some control.

I came back from overseas with all these wonderful ideas, but Dad was in charge, and I didn't get to implement those ideas. It wasn't my business, and there wasn't any discussion about how that sort of input and change might have occurred.

We examine family charters and building family governance in this step because we're trying to sort out the 'family stuff' and the 'business stuff' and ensure that each individual – who is on their own life journey – is well taken care of in the discussions, while also seeing if there is a business to be passed from one generation to the next, and how that next generation will transition into ownership, leadership, and running the business.

Why you need a family charter

When we are creating a family charter, we're covering a range of topics:

- What is the preferred retirement age of the current generation – when do they want to exit?
- What are their plans for transitioning out, and how is this going to be handled?

- Who in the next generation is taking over? Is it going to be one sibling, or is there a case for co-managing directors?
- What skills do family members have, and how is the business going to support these family members in building their skills?
- What is the strategy of the business and what are our aspirations for it – where are we looking to be and what are we building on?

We have a family group, but we also have a business with certain needs. We have to attend to both of those things. You can't just have someone take over as CEO because they are the oldest sibling if they don't have the skill set to shepherd the business to success.

Equally, while parents might have a desire for the kids to take over the family business, it is not a good approach to force a business down the throats of kids who just don't want to do that.

In the farming industry in Australia over the last two generations, we've seen the loss of many family-owned and -run businesses and the rise of corporate-owned farms, partly because kids saw that owning and running a farm was just too hard and they didn't want to work that hard for seemingly little return. Even in the last decade, the number of dairy farms – a bastion of family ownership in the past – has dropped from over 6000 farms to just 4400.

I have seen situations where two siblings take on co-CEO roles. I've also seen situations where the children of owners are not settled in their own lives, with grandkids perhaps having trouble at school or personal financial struggles, and so the kids have trouble focusing on the family business.

The intentions of the current generation are important to communicate.

What if the parents decide all of a sudden that they want out and choose to sell the business?

Every business should always be sale-ready, and it is up to the owners, but how does that impact the kids?

Should the decision be made to go intergenerational, that starts off a process of inviting the kids to come and work in the business. Maybe that starts as holiday or after-school work, and then later something more formal. Yet the questions still need to be posed: do you want to take over the business at some stage? From the kids, it might be, do you want me to take over this business from you at some stage, and when might that be?

We need to deal with expectations, needs, thoughts, desires and ideas in both generations, and with each individual and their partners in each generation too.

When we are talking about the family charter, we're talking about the family, what we want to do together, our aspirations and vision for the business, role clarity, and who the boss is. We need to think about communication between family members and who needs to know what and when. How do we handle conflict? These sorts of things.

I've mentioned the three areas of family, business and ownership. Depending on which circles a family member is in will determine the sort of communication they need to receive, and this all has to be agreed.

Remember, the more communication and the more agreement you can foster, the better the outcome for the family, for the business, and for each individual. Everyone needs to be heard, understood, and have agreements and decisions made.

In some families – take the Murdoch family, for instance – whether or not one of those members is working in the business, they still represent the family every time they go out in public. The same could be true of your family in the community in which you operate.

Generally, in a family business, the current owners will be making the decisions, but what we are looking for is a willingness of family members to sit down, communicate and make decisions about the family charter, the business and the changing roles over time.

Sometimes I see the next generation champing at the bit because they've been promised a more substantive role in running the business but the parents can't let go. The more you sit down and agree, the less these sorts of situations will occur, because everyone is on the same page.

You don't want a situation where an adult child thinks to themselves they've wasted 30 years of their life waiting to take over the family business, only for the parents to renege on their deal or, worse still, die before preparations are made.

Managing change over time

We're trying to synchronise business and family governance as the business grows and transitions from generation to generation. When a business is started, you're usually dealing with a single family – Mum, Dad, and maybe even no kids. Then the kids come along, grow up, and the business grows and transitions down a generation or two, and suddenly you find yourself with a complicated family tree, with various branches and multiple business units. The sort of governance you need at the start is very different from that needed a generation or two down the line.

We might start with a simple family charter. Then later, we might end up with a family council representing ownership. We might start with Mum and Dad being the board, but then need an advisory board and later on a formal board.

So the idea is to establish the correct governance structure for the family and the business, depending on the size of the family and the complexity and size of the business.

Once a business starts to become more complex, that is a point where you probably start separating out different structures for different types of decisions. You can have a family ownership council of shareholders, a board with family representation, or the family employs a board and then directs the board to deliver certain results from the business for the family.

Circumstances change over time, and different generations can bring new skills or new understandings of technology to the table to help transform businesses over time.

I visited a marble factory in Norway that had for many years been successful at mining and crushing their marble to provide a glossy surface for paper – like you might see in National Geographic. This business isn't as popular as it used to be, but now the mines of this company are being set up by the current generation as data centres – because the mines offer a great protected and temperature-controlled environment.

This sort of transition can occur in any business over time, so within the discussions of transition from one generation to another, and getting the right family members doing the right roles in the business, we're also continually looking at business strategy and keeping the business current, valued and successful in its markets.

We often see family businesses branch out into multiple different businesses, so in building for the next generation, we also have the complexity of multiple businesses with multiple income streams potentially including passive investments such as property portfolios. You can see why governance for the family and for the business is critical to get right and to transform the structure over time to keep up with family dynamics and business dynamics.

> The needs and strategy of the family and the needs and strategy of the business are complementary yet different.

Our aim in the BUILD phase is to find harmony between what the family and individual family members want to achieve in the next phase of their lives, and the role the business plays in helping them and the whole family achieve those goals.

No one wants a hospital pass

Strategy in the BUILD phase is fundamentally important. We need to know the business is robust and can continue to grow under the stewardship of the next generation.

Stewardship is the foundation that holds up the structure of the family business. It is the mindset that the business is not simply owned, but temporarily cared for – nurtured for the benefit of future generations. While strategy determines *where* the business is going, stewardship is about *why* it matters that the business endures. It ensures that decisions are made not just for short-term profit, but with a long-term vision that respects the business's history, honours its values, and sustains its legacy. Without stewardship, strategy becomes a house built without a foundation – impressive at first, but vulnerable to collapse over time.

No one wants a hospital pass. Taking over a dying business helps no one. So this is a critical part of planning and decision-making too. What business are we in? Are we diversifying into new areas? How do we have to adapt to keep the business successful? Will it require us to invest in new plant and equipment? How do the current and next generation feel about those risks and opportunities?

Here are some questions you could be asking yourself at this point if you are in the generation that is going to take over the business:

- Does your family have a governance structure that meets its needs?
- Do you make family decisions and business decisions together? Why?
- Who makes the decisions?
- Do you have a family council or similar group that meets to make these decisions?
- Do you have a strategy in place for the business to protect, grow and manage risks?
- Do you have a trusted independent adviser to whom you can turn for help with your decisions?

There are many other questions you might ask yourself when considering taking over a business. Do you want to live in the same city as your parents to run the business? Are you getting married and having kids? What are your lifestyle goals? Do you even *want* to run the family business?

Gaining clarity on how business works

A strong family charter doesn't just define roles and values – it also ensures that everyone, regardless of their background or experience, understands how the business itself actually works.

Before a family can govern or guide a business together, they need a shared foundation of business basics. Whether you make something or offer a service, the four things that exist in every business are:

1. making a sale
2. producing or supplying your service or product
3. invoicing for the work or product
4. collecting the money.

Everything we do in business revolves around these four simple steps. Universities and colleges exist to teach us how to do this.

We have accountants who watch the money.

We have lawyers who work with the rules.

We have engineers who design the products.

We have skills that, when taught, improve the productivity of those who have a natural affinity for any of these steps.

Gaining clarity on how *your* business works

Once we have some clarity on how business works, we need to understand how *our own* business operates. Our business is unique. Our people are unique. And our way of supplying our products or services is unique.

This presents one of our major challenges: learning how our business does what it does so we can be better than others and maintain or grow our market share.

And we must understand our family and how we interact too! As much as we might want the family to understand each other and work together, we may not all be able to manage the challenges that arise from being in such close proximity for long periods.

While we may have lived with other family members for years, we don't necessarily know how they think – especially at work – which sometimes leads us to make statements or decisions without due consideration or consultation when necessary.

We also need to understand that you can't win every battle every time.

> Sometimes being 'right' does not lead to the best decision for the individual, the family or the business.

In the UNITE step, you captured your family values – a shared understanding of your purpose. You now have a group of individual family members who have shared their goals, dreams, needs and wants. You understand each other better, how you work together, and the purpose of your business.

Now we enter the next stage of the process: BUILD.

Creating a family charter

In essence, what you want to achieve in the BUILD step is to align your family with the business. We're aiming for a situation where each family member understands their role in the business. Part of this understanding will also involve creating a set of 'rules for living' that each family member agrees to follow.

Philosophically, we're now talking about governance.

Governance – by definition – encompasses the system by which an organisation is controlled and operates, and the mechanisms by which it, and its people, are held to account.

In the case of a family business, we achieve this by creating a family charter.

While not legally binding in most countries, including Australia, a family charter is essential for setting values, defining the purpose of the family's involvement in the business, and establishing guidelines for hiring, firing and conflict resolution. Your family charter will evolve over time because it needs to reflect your family's current circumstances and intentions and be clear on its agreements.

One important personal value that I hold in helping families create a charter is that I never write it for them. I'll facilitate discussions, and collect ideas and thoughts from the family in a whiteboard session.

But the words have to be yours.

Why?

If the charter is in your words – the family's words – then it is real for you, much more likely to be etched in your hearts and minds, and more likely to inspire you as a family. It's also more likely to hold weight when it comes to you or another family member being accountable for any actions they might take.

I could write a formal charter clause that states:

> All family members shall perform their duties in accordance with their designated roles and responsibilities and shall refrain from any conduct that may be construed as dereliction or misappropriation of business resources.

But a family that writes something like this ...

> As a family, we recognise that not performing our role in the business, taking unwarranted time off, doing other things on work time, or not achieving the results for which we are responsible, is as much stealing as if we put our hands in the till at the front counter.

... is far more likely to embrace the idea that just because you are family doesn't mean you can shirk the responsibility of your role as a salesperson, accountant, operations manager or other position. If you do shirk these roles, you are putting the business in danger and stealing from it.

I once encountered a family where one sibling wasn't performing, and actually withdrew money from a parent's bank account without consent. This required an intervention from the other siblings. Situations like this erode trust, destabilise the business, and cause long-term damage to both the company and the family relationships that underpin it. A family charter can help you deal with such situations.

Getting started on the charter

There are many ways you can create a charter. Here is an example.

This image outlines a six-step process for drafting a family charter or family governance policies. The process begins with **education and best practices**, where key governance principles are shared to establish a common understanding. This is followed by **information gathering**, which involves exploring family members' perspectives, hopes and concerns. **Facilitated drafting meetings** are then held to evaluate policy options and reach consensus. In the draft **policies/family charter** stage, an adviser or family member prepares an initial draft. The **review working drafts and** iterate stage involves feedback and revisions, and finally, the process concludes with **approve and implement**, where the family formally endorses and adopts the final version.

01
Education and best practices
Share family governance best practices and key concepts to ensure common understanding

02
Information gathering
To understand family enterprise, family member perspectives, hopes and concerns

03
Facilitated drafting meetings
Workshops with family members to evaluate pros and cons of policy options and reach consensus

04
Draft policies/family charter
Advisor or family volunteer drafts initial version of policy

05
Review working drafts and iterate
Family reviews draft policies and provides feedback

06
Approve and implement
Family formally endorses and adopts the final version

Some families start with a brief document, while larger or more complex families or businesses may develop a more detailed charter.

When you're working on a family charter, it can be useful to designate one person in the family as the champion for the charter. They organise meetings with each family member who is involved. They facilitate discussions and help craft the words, refining them with input from the family.

This idea of appointing a champion for a task or project works well in all fields of endeavour, and your family charter is no different. Otherwise, it could end up in that parable that goes something like this:

> Somebody, everybody, anybody and nobody got together and agreed that they should go ahead and plough the fields ready for planting. The weather was starting to turn, and if the ploughing wasn't done, they wouldn't be able to plant in time for the spring rains.
>
> Unfortunately, everybody was sure that somebody was going to do it, and anybody could have done it, but nobody did. Somebody got angry at that because it was everybody's job. Everybody thought anybody could do it, but nobody realised that everybody wouldn't do it. In the end, everybody blamed somebody when nobody did what anybody could have.

Anyway ...

Let's move on!

The creation of a family charter will provide you with a structured way to facilitate discussions about the family's vision and operational policies. I encourage you – or the family champion, as the case may be – to have regular meetings to review and refine the charter.

These gatherings can also become events where different generations interact, allowing younger family members to learn from their elders. Gatherings don't have to be onerous, and the family charter discussion could be just a workshop during a long weekend beach break or resort holiday with the family once a year.

You can decide as a family to rotate the champion role or keep it with one person.

A whiteboard session where the champion asks strategic questions of each family member will gather valuable input, both when creating the charter and for keeping it up to date. The exact questions matter less than the territory they cover – but here are some essential ones to include:

- What values are most important to us as a family, and how should they be reflected in the business?
- How will we communicate with each other about business matters – formally, informally, and when conflict arises?
- How often should we review and update the family charter, and who will be responsible for this?
- What is the core purpose of our business, beyond profit?
- How will we decide who takes on which roles within the business?
- How will family members be remunerated, and how will we ensure this is fair and sustainable?
- What expectations do we have for training and educating family members for their roles?
- What will we do if a family member is not able to perform in their role or meet the agreed expectations?

Your charter can also address specific policies, such as financial support for education or homeownership for younger generations.

I've seen examples where some families choose to include philanthropy as a shared mission, setting up foundations or structured giving programmes that align with their values.

I've worked with families where there is a section of the charter that describes how the family can support other business ventures by family members. If a member expresses interest in starting a business, the family may choose to provide financial backing if they see promise in the venture.

Keeping the charter up to date

There's more than one way to keep a charter alive and relevant.

I've seen a software tool developed by one family for the purpose of keeping a charter up to date. It is now used by several families around Australia for that purpose. This could be particularly useful if you have a family that is dispersed around the globe and physical get-togethers are difficult to organise. The software is like a private social media network, where only family members have access.

> The process of building a family charter is ongoing, requires regular discussions, and your family will adjust it over time to contend with change.

This could be a change in the family, such as the death of a matriarch, or it could be a change in the business adapting to market trends.

Just a caution before this family charter becomes an unmanageable 'beast' of a document: *avoid overreach*. The primary focus of a family charter is guiding principles for the family, not operational business details. You don't want to 'get into the weeds' in a family charter in an attempt to also make it a strategic and operational plan for the business itself. That document would not need to include the entire family – it would be generated by the family members who hold executive roles in the business, under the direction of the board of directors.

Yes, it might include family members in each of these roles, but equally, the family might employ someone as CEO who is not a family member. The board then puts in place a guide on what they want the business to achieve in terms of revenue, growth, profit and more. Then the executive team implements plans to achieve those overall goals, within the defining purpose of the business set down by the family.

You can't have everybody trying to do everything or being involved in everything. This will lead to a top-heavy, or in this case a 'family-heavy', operating system.

When you get into third and fourth generation families, you can have a lot of people involved. Sometimes there might be an overarching charter, but then branches of the family can also develop their own specific charters, covering their interests and activities.

A friend of mine recently shared a story with me about a family that has evolved into two operating branches. While the founder and his family were initially involved in dairy farming, the sibling brothers have extended this into two very specific business interests. One stayed in dairy and added health foods to the mix. The other brother moved into natural health products. While the brothers remain close, each of their families could potentially have their own charter covering these different areas of focus.

Aligning family governance with business governance

In my experience, some families do not know what they do not know. Through structured conversations, they can gain clarity on their values, purpose and long-term goals. A family charter serves as a framework for your discussions, ensuring your family remains aligned and proactive in its approach to governance and decision-making.

One of the key challenges in family businesses is aligning family governance with business governance. The structure of governance evolves from the early days of a small family-run operation, where perhaps just your parents were making the decisions.

When the business gets bigger and more family members become involved, it can become necessary to have more formal structures with advisory boards or even full boards of directors.

Family governance should ideally support business decisions, especially in matters like investments and resource allocation, ensuring that family interests are respected without disrupting the operational needs of the business. An example of this might be where the family has dictated that they need to achieve a 20% return from the business each year. This could influence poor short-term behaviour by those running the business to drive profit at the expense of long-term viability. You could sell off a lot of stock to achieve a number in one year and then find you've artificially influenced the figures. This can also occur if you don't get the method of remunerating executives, such as your CEO, right. If they are measured and receive their bonuses based on a particular metric, they may begin operating for the bonus, not the business.

> It is crucial for families to view their business as an investment, especially when family members are shareholders.

You want to assess the business's performance against alternative investments like bank deposits or the stock market to ensure it generates sufficient returns.

It might be better for some families to invest their money in alternative vehicles if the business is not generating equitable returns. It is good to encourage yourself and family members to evaluate the business critically and consider its long-term financial sustainability.

Consider how you can create a balance between family needs and business operations, particularly when it comes to extracting value from the business.

I believe this is critical.

You may have family members who need funds for personal reasons, but these financial demands should be balanced with the business's growth and capital needs. A clear governance structure, ideally with a board clearly being a balance point, helps ensure that both family and business interests are aligned.

Preserving and growing family wealth

As family businesses transition through generations, education becomes vital in managing the family's interests. This is the sort of education that isn't really taught at school. That is the topic of wealth management, the value of money, and how to preserve and grow family wealth.

In my experience, and in researching the topic of family business, there is a distinct difference between the ways corporations and family-run businesses operate.

Family-run businesses are known to think more long-term than corporations.

Family businesses that have lasted two or more generations are often more focused on long-term wealth creation than short-term 'profit' or 'dividend' considerations. Not to say these two ideas aren't linked, but family businesses are more likely to prioritise investment in the future to create wealth over a single year's EBIT or dividend figures.

I was speaking with a colleague the other day who referred to a family-owned and -operated manufacturing business. Despite being under short-term pressure from imported and cheaper products in their market, this family has stuck with their values of innovation and investment.

At this moment, even though it doesn't make sense for the profit figures they desire, they are investing heavily in research with an Australian university on a novel concept that could completely change the way the industry and its customers approach the use of their products. It has global implications and could dramatically improve the sustainability of their product.

While I'm deliberately being vague about this industry segment to preserve their anonymity, there is nothing vague about a tenfold decrease in costs, with an orders-of-magnitude improvement in sustainability in this market if their research pays off.

While it's not impossible, I see this kind of values-led business investment for long-term gain – for the family as shareholders, but also for the planet – as being beyond the ability and even understanding of most corporates who are chasing short-term dividends.

Anyway, back to my point about education.

You need to invest in educating the next generation – your children, your nieces and nephews, any family member involved in the family business – about wealth management. Don't foster a situation where any family member sees the business as their personal piggy bank. This is far more common than you think.

We have all heard the saying that in family business:

> The first generation builds the business, the second generation maintains it, and the third generation squanders it.

Most family businesses struggle to maintain success beyond the third generation due to changes in the drive and focus of each generation.

It isn't always true, of course, but the solution to it, and the source of success for those businesses that defy this, is that they have tools and processes to maintain and foster focus and innovation, and they inevitably have strong leaders in each generation.

Leadership, like wealth management, is not always a skill learned from textbooks, so it is essential for each generation in charge of a business to invest in educating their offspring and relatives about business, wealth, the value of money, and how to preserve and grow wealth over time.

This education will help prepare them for future leadership roles within the family business and ensure they understand the business's operations and goals. Without proper guidance, the younger generation may inherit wealth without understanding how to manage it, leading to poor financial decisions.

If you are reading this book and you belong to that generation about to take over the family business, and you haven't received this education, make that a priority for yourself right now. And nothing should stop you from investing in your own skills in these areas – even if this hasn't been offered by your parents.

It isn't common to see people with strong education in these areas, but it is common sense to acquire those skills. I believe it is an imperative and critical part of your personal toolkit if you want to successfully transition this business and see yourself, your parents and your relatives prosper in the future.

Leadership development

I also want to explore the idea of leadership development and succession planning with you. While we're not at the transition phase yet and there is work to be done before we get there, the topic of succession planning should start as soon as someone is identified as a 'potential successor', as preparing for this role may take several years.

When I was a young man, my father offered me an opportunity to go overseas and work for a family-operated business in the timber industry. I've noted elsewhere the personal impact this had on me – I loved the experience and I still recall with fondness the environment where I worked, which has to be one of the most beautiful places on the planet.

From a professional perspective, the experience exposed me to different elements of our industry. I learned a lot about the business of timber while I was overseas, and when I returned, I was more knowledgeable and better able to think about our business operations and see opportunities using that experience.

Below is a model of leadership development and succession planning.

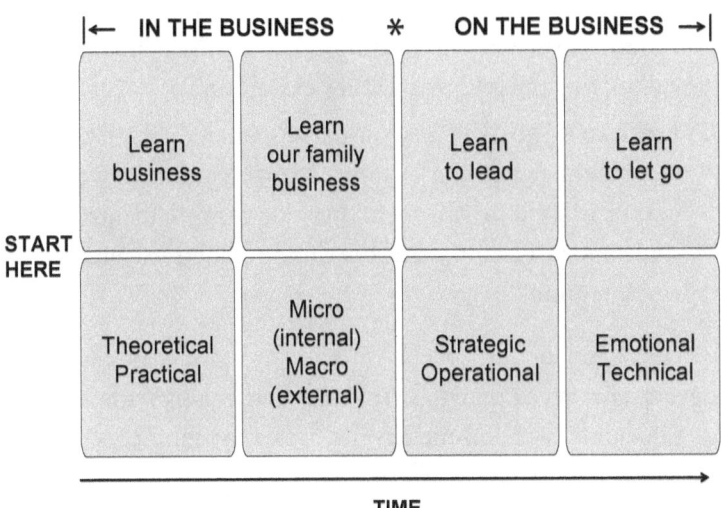

This model outlines a four-phase journey for next-generation leaders in a family business, structured across two axes: **strategic vs operational** and **emotional vs technical**. It also contrasts **macro (external)** and **micro (internal)** perspectives, and distinguishes between working **on** the business and working **in** it:

1. **Learn business:** The journey begins with understanding the fundamentals of business itself – both the external, macro-level context (such as market trends and competitive positioning) and the internal, operational workings (like systems, processes, and daily routines).
2. **Learn our family business:** The focus then shifts to the unique DNA of the family enterprise. This includes

its values, legacy, governance structures, and the subtle interpersonal dynamics that distinguish it from a non-family business.

3. **Learn to lead:** Having grasped the 'what' and 'why', the emerging leader now develops the skills to lead – strategically and operationally. This phase includes building confidence in decision-making, guiding others, and embodying the leadership ethos of the family.
4. **Learn to let go:** The final quadrant – often directed at the incumbent generation – emphasises the emotional work of transition. It involves relinquishing control, mentoring successors, and supporting the shift in leadership with trust and intention.

The direction of movement through the model is clockwise, suggesting a developmental sequence that begins with business fundamentals and culminates in a healthy intergenerational transition.

It starts with learning the business. For many families, this can entail someone from the next generation heading off to work in the broader industry – in other words, *not* in the family business.

There is much to commend in this approach, as it puts the individual in a situation where they have to learn and fend for themselves in a role in the industry. There is no family safety net, and their personal skills, abilities and successes – along with a promotion or two – can help them build confidence that they can succeed in their chosen profession – even if this profession is just one part of the overall family business and the market in which it operates.

Technical skill comes before leadership skill, as I will show.

In this first step, the family member will learn about macroeconomic issues like the dynamics of the market or industry trends, and they will learn micro-level skills such as internal operations and the day-to-day activities of running a business.

With this experience under their belt, the individual might return to tackle step 2 of the process, which is to learn the family business, or 'learning ours'. This development of skills and experience will have the specific values, systems and practices that make your family business unique as the guideposts for the individual.

Having learnt *the* business and *our* business, the individual can then enter a phase of learning to lead. Leadership is the step-up phase of our development as business owners, and many business owners never make the leap from 'technical skills' of working *in* the business to the general management and leadership skills of working *on* the business. It is my strong belief that this is the reason so many businesses only ever employ the owner, or just a few staff.

Without the ability to lead, you can't employ people to follow you.

This phase of learning to lead – step 3 – involves the practicalities of becoming a decision-maker, whether in strategic planning or daily management. If we want our family business to last for generations, we have to foster this transition of not only the business but also create a family dynasty of 'a leader for every generation'.

I would have liked to think it was me at the time when my father died, but in truth, the best leader at that time was my sister. She understood the business from the top down, while my skills at the time were more operational.

Over time, I learned and developed my skills, so that when I was ready to buy the family business from my family, I was indeed ready to lead that business.

Succession planning

One of the most challenging aspects of family business succession is the emotional difficulty that comes with letting go.

Many parents – and yours may be in this situation – identify strongly with their role within the business. When it comes time to think about passing the baton, they can find it deeply challenging, not only regarding their role but their entire existence. Letting go of control and passing leadership to the next generation requires not only trust but also a shift in identity.

There has to be a deliberate exit strategy, and you have to plan for generational transition. We handle much of this planning within the BUILD phase, as it is indelibly intertwined with the strategy of the business.

We're not doing the transition yet, but you can see that a lot of planning – and not a little time – might be put into preparing the younger generation to take over.

As well as helping parents let go and allowing that takeover to occur.

We want a win for parents and a win for children. That can be tough to achieve, but you can do it with forethought, courage, communication, planning and commitment. A robust structure allows the next generation to step up and lead effectively, without disrupting the business's continuity or the family's legacy.

We are taking the key steps towards ensuring that family members and the business are aligned in terms of governance, values and leadership. We're preparing the next generation to take over the business, inherit wealth, and then manage and grow it responsibly. Education, successful planning, and acknowledging and handling the emotional aspects of leadership transitions will help you sustain a successful family business over time.

Businesses can be funny beasts – not funny ha-ha but funny strange. A business can face change or decline due to external factors such as economic shifts or technological advancements. No one makes buggy whips any more.

If you've taken the time to understand both the family and business dynamics before moving forward with succession planning, you'll be in a better position to succeed.

Aligning the family and business strategy

Every business faces change, and business strategy is a way of achieving desirable ends with available means.

A generational family business is likely to encounter wave after wave of change, and last long enough to see new customers emerge and new technologies deployed in designing, manufacturing, and distributing products and services. Governments will come and go.

A key part of the BUILD phase is for the family to work with their executives and staff to ensure there is a robust strategy in place to manage all of this.

In my own family business, we were in timber merchandising and sawmills. The sawmilling is virtually nonexistent today. But I observed our family business adapt across three generations. My grandfather made boxes from timber, then bought a timber mill, then expanded into trucks, a Ford dealership, and construction. We were what is called 'vertically and horizontally integrated', and each division was added to bolster business performance over time. When timber stopped being used to pack fruit, my grandfather got into cardboard box making.

What is critical in your business strategy?

Your family, and depending on the size of your business, your board and executives must know the current state of the industry. They need to know what factors are driving success and what will restrain you from success. Family businesses must be prepared to adapt to changing circumstances, whether it's market conditions, technological innovations like artificial intelligence, or other external factors.

How does this affect the family?

There is kind of a feedback loop between the family and its needs and values, and the business and its needs and operational issues.

I've seen families that have had to 'prune the family tree' because the business can no longer support the size of the family from a financial or wealth perspective, or sometimes the family members want to diverge.

It is sometimes necessary, but nevertheless challenging, for families to go through a process of reducing family involvement in the business when it no longer aligns with the family's or the business's goals. This can lead to tensions, legal disputes and difficult decisions.

This is where your family charter comes in, and clear communication about how decisions are made is an essential tool to navigate these complexities.

So, businesses need to constantly evaluate their short- and long-term plans.

I've seen businesses with 12-month, five-year and even 10-year horizons, but I'm the first to acknowledge that in today's climate, some industries are difficult to predict more than a year out due to rapid technological changes.

Governments also play a significant role in these transitions by mandating changes like electric vehicles and renewable energy sources, which can affect industries and business strategies.

Shareholding and decision-making powers

In the BUILD phase, we're highlighting the importance of balancing the needs of the business with the family's goals.

> In some cases, individuals within the family may not fit the business model, and difficult decisions need to be made to ensure harmony and success in both your business and your family relationships.

Shareholding and decision-making powers are dynamics in the ownership of a business. These need to be taken into account to avoid issues of favouritism or unequal power dynamics.

What would happen if one owner of a business had two children, and the other had three? Do they get equal shares across the board – 20% each, or does each family get 50% and then it gets split within the family? In this case, the children of one parent have a 25% share each, but the children of the other family only have 16.67%. Will this cause a situation of unequal power among cousins?

The duration of each of these phases – UNITE, BUILD and TRANSITION – will vary depending on your family, your business, and the complexities involved. However, it should not be rushed.

Unfortunately, I've had to advise families where a sudden event, such as the death of the owner and founder, has forced rapid and uncontrolled change.

If you have the time, take the time.

A generational 'cake' takes time to bake.

For the next generation of owners of a family business – of which you are likely one – it is crucial that you ask questions and gain a deep understanding of the family business, from roles and responsibilities to ownership structures.

These discussions should not just focus on the immediate business needs but also on what the business means for the family in the long term. Ask questions about the business, how you fit in, what role you and your siblings are going to play, what roles they want to play, what skills you'll need, and what challenges you will face – physically, emotionally and structurally – in making the transition.

Time to BUILD

All this should be done before the transition is even contemplated. It is about the questions, questions, questions. Finding answers for each and evaluating what those answers mean for each family member and the business you all run together.

External events, like illness, death or market disruptions, may accelerate the need for transition planning. Flexibility in responding to unexpected changes while maintaining clear communication and a well-structured plan is critical for family business sustainability. Being well prepared not only reduces stress and confusion in times of crisis, but also allows the family to respond with confidence and unity, protecting both relationships and the long-term viability of the business.

Families involved in business need to make informed, strategic decisions about the future. Open communication, followed by thorough planning and having the flexibility to navigate challenges and transitions, will ensure that you and the family and your business will thrive in the long term.

As you progress through the BUILD stage, you are looking for the following outcomes for yourself and the family. You'll be ready to move on to the TRANSITION phase when these things have been achieved:

- You have a set of family rules to live and work by – a family charter.
- You have some stability, focus, clarity, and understanding of your business with a clear path forward – a business strategy with visible opportunities for the business.
- You have evolved your family unity into unity and purpose for the business.
- You have a family champion for the charter – with the possibility of rotating this role within the family to keep this charter fresh, current, and useful for the family.
- You understand the ownership of the business – who owns shares, or if the business is in a trust or partnership, what the differences are and how they affect each family member.

Exercise: Clarifying the BUILD Stage

If you've progressed through the BUILD stage successfully, you should now:

- understand the difference between working in the business and building the business
- have initiated or developed a family charter
- be developing a clear business strategy for the next generation
- have begun conversations about ownership, leadership and education
- be aligning family governance with business governance.

Let's bring this into focus.

1. What is one key insight you've gained about the difference between being an employee and being an owner of the business?

   ....
   ....
   ....
   ....

2. List three topics your family charter needs to address in more detail:

   ....
   ....

3. What does your family business strategy look like for the next three to five years? Write one or two clear priorities.

　　..
　　..
　　..
　　..
　　..

4. Do you know who currently owns the business? Who holds decision-making power?

　　..
　　..
　　..
　　..
　　..

5. Reflect: What new conversations have started (or need to start) in your family as a result of the BUILD stage?

　　..
　　..
　　..
　　..
　　..

STEP 3

STEP 3

TRANSITION
from one generation to the next

> *'A prudent person profits from personal experience, a wise one from the experience of others.'*
> Dr Joseph Collins, family business strategist and trusted adviser to multi-generational enterprises

People around the world have heard of the concept of the hero's journey.

Every hero's journey has a purpose and challenges to overcome.

In the hero's journey, there is always a guide – be it Yoda, Gandalf, or Mr Miyagi.

In our journey together, we have reached the main purpose of this book: to guide the transition of your family business from one generation to the next.

There is a difference on this journey.

Being multi-generational, there are many heroes.

Every member of your family is a heroine or hero because the transition of a family business is a challenge; it involves a lot of work and can be frustrating.

It is challenging because there are a lot of moving parts, and potentially a lot of people to help win throughout the process.

The transition will not be perfect, but we can make it better, easier and more rewarding for each individual, the whole family, and for the business as well – if we're willing to do the work, invest the time, and talk.

> Having good communication remains the single most important thing you can do throughout this entire journey.

If we take the analogy of a bushwalk on a mountain path where visibility is only a few metres in any direction, for all of your walking party to make the journey safely, each person can contribute their information and opinions on the area they can see. Together, you may well be able to see the entire path, or even the entire mountain.

Bringing it all together

Before we move ahead, let's view the path behind us and celebrate how far you've come on this journey so far.

If the UNITE step has been navigated successfully, you have written family values, you understand why you are better together, you have some clarity on what the family wants to achieve, and the purpose of the family business.

In the BUILD step, you've broadened your family guidebook from values into a complete charter, which includes the rules by which the family will operate and how the family will engage with the business. In the business, you've put together a clear strategy on a time horizon of a few years at least. You've identified the roles each family member might play, and you might have even started them on their journey of learning the business or starting education. You have focus and stability, and the opportunity for your family business is clear.

In the TRANSITION phase, we start to bring all this work together.

We have all the puzzle pieces, and we know the final image.

We understand what each generation wants out of the transition.

You may not know exactly when a particular event, such as retirement or role transition, will occur, but you have a rough timeline in mind.

Your family is meeting regularly to discuss the issues of family values, the family charter, roles and responsibilities, and even ownership of the business.

The challenges of transition

The transition of a family business can be tough for a number of very understandable reasons:

- The founders are heavily invested in the business, and often the business becomes an integral part of their personal identity – it's tough to let go, and tough to see that someone else can do a job as well as you can – family or not.
- The next generation wants to make their mark and can chafe against the structure and fixed ideas of the previous generation on what will work in the business.

- Often, neither generation communicates their ideas, thoughts, feelings and expectations enough to ensure everyone is operating from the same page.
- Despite assurances and promises, the timeframe of change and expectations can be different from generation to generation, father to daughter, mother to son.
- The business itself has to deal with change, all while this is going on.
- Founders can be in preservation mode, thinking about retirement and protecting assets as they see the finish line approach. The finish line isn't even on the mind of the next generation, who are willing to take more risks because they have no set time limit.
- For the next generation to take over, they might need years of education and on-the-job training. Most people, family or not, rarely look that far into the future.

So how do we make transition easier?

We break down all the actions into smaller, more approachable steps.

You will have already done a lot of the required work in the UNITE and BUILD steps, but there will still be a long road ahead of you to effect the transition successfully.

Ownership

Let's talk about ownership for a brief moment to underline just one reason why transition can take some time. Let's keep the example simple and say that Mum and Dad own the business. They have mortgaged their house to invest in the business. Perhaps you and your siblings don't have enough money yet to buy the business outright at a fair value.

How are Mum and Dad going to separate the house and business and get the mortgage paid off if they retire?

Will they instead leave the business in their will, and will ownership transition be handled when deaths occur?

How many shares are going to go to each sibling?

In a big family, there may be a potential share transfer to a family member who isn't going to work in the business, and more shares to someone who is. How are these two shareholders going to communicate when their roles are different? Are their expectations going to be different?

On business roles, what if two siblings want to take over the CEO role from Mum, but one of them is better qualified or better suited to the role? How will you decide who takes over? Will you rotate the CEO role?

We still have to handle the issues of governance. We need aligned plans for the family and the business, for ownership and operation of the business. We still need to communicate.

As the actual activities of transition begin to be implemented, it is possible issues will arise that you have not thought of previously, or people may start to get nervous now that the transition is real and not some theoretical future event written in a document.

> You need to ensure that your generation and the one before you, who runs the business right now, are in good communication.

I hope we've established that in the UNITE phase, but you still might have unexpressed things that need to be raised and handled.

In my experience, many transitions are poorly planned, and there are misunderstandings about roles and expectations. This isn't easy.

Sometimes, people in your generation who are taking over feel a deep responsibility to their parents, and even though they didn't really want to take over, they go through with it, only to find that a lack of passion or interest leads to failure.

Some kids – and when I say kids, I could be talking about 50-year-olds – start to take over the business but are continually stifled in their actions by a parent who just can't let go.

So you need to really assess your passion and ability to make this transition. It is in your interests, your parents' interests, and the interests of the business.

I think sometimes it helps to think of a business as an entity of its own – with its own needs and wants. It is a better way than having the identity of the business confused with your own. This is what happens when a founder can't let go – the business is too much a part of their identity that they can't separate it.

If there are multiple heirs involved, are there good dynamics and communication between all of you?

Can you see taking over and working well with your sisters or cousins? One of them as the CFO, you as the head of sales, and your sister as CEO?

Would that work?

I've spoken about next-generation family members gaining experience in 'the business' before returning to 'our business'. This can be invaluable. Imagine three siblings working in three different businesses related to the family business. Coming back after some success and combining your knowledge to make the family business super successful.

Wouldn't that be amazing?

Nice, but if you absolutely can't stand your cousin, how could you work professionally with them and let them control the finances?

External experience can build self-esteem, knowledge and skills, but family dynamics is a separate challenge that requires communication, planning and forethought.

I've worked with some businesses where one or two out of the brood actually decide not to be a part of the transition. They went elsewhere while one of the brothers took over. Everyone was happy, and that business is still running very successfully under the son's guidance. This would not have been the case if the other siblings had gone against their own ideas and thoughts and tried to stick with it, even though it wasn't their passion.

Family and business dynamics

> The actual transition is a complicated mix of family and business dynamics.

Don't get me wrong – *complicated* doesn't mean *impossible*.

You just need the right tools to break down the plan into approachable actions.

Josh Barron and Rob Lachenauer have developed what they call a Four-Room Model, which helps you separate family dynamics from business operations and allows for clearer responsibilities and relationships.

A simple example of this is that you may have family as shareholders only, or shareholders and members of a board, or shareholders, members of a board and having operational responsibility in the business. Or any mix of these roles. But they are all in the 'family room', just not in some or all of the other rooms. When you consider the idea of being in a room and being involved in the actions of that room, it also makes it easier to realise the rooms you are *not* a part of, and therefore clarifies your individual sphere of influence and responsibility.

Don't forget, you also have your family charter, which is an agreed set of rules by which the family operates as a family and in relationship with the business. An agreed guidebook will bring you back to the right path when you stray, or are diverted by some 'shiny object' or opportunity that doesn't fit with your plans. You might even be knocked off the right path by an unexpected market event or the death of a key family member.

As long as you have your plans, and as long as you have an agreement to communicate openly and regularly, you, your family and your business will be fine.

It's not rocket science.

Some might say the complexity of rocket science pales into insignificance beside family science, and maybe they are right.

However, time and time again, the right tools, the right agreements and the right willingness to communicate have resulted in success for the families I've worked with.

I believe they will work for you too.

Communication

Trust is the foundation of any successful family business, and clear, consistent communication is one of the most effective ways to build and maintain it. Trust doesn't just appear – it's cultivated through openness, reliability and ongoing dialogue. Having clear and structured communication protocols will help you mitigate potential conflicts and reinforce the sense that everyone has a voice and a role in the conversation.

You'll find that the more often the family meets, the easier it gets. Trust grows when people feel heard and understood. If you keep the pipes clean in your house, a blockage is unlikely and the pressure can't build up. Similarly, if you block communication or don't create opportunities for it to flow, you will see pressure – in the form of disagreements or differing expectations – build up in the family.

Regular, honest communication not only diffuses tension but also sends a clear signal: we trust each other enough to talk, to listen, and to work through things together.

A great example of this might be an annual target for the business to make, let's say, $250,000 in profit. The family has agreed that a percentage of profit is always distributed as a dividend. Let's say the family doesn't meet for two quarters because of some scheduling clashes. One family member with a 10% share in the business is expecting around $25,000 in dividends and they've gone ahead and 'spent' the money in advance of the company's end-of-year results. But an unexpected loss of a major customer in the last quarter has wiped out half the profit. No one knows because the family hasn't met. Now someone in the family, who is a shareholder but not working in the business, gets an unwanted surprise.

It's a simple example, but you can see how a lack of communication can cause a breakdown, upset or unfulfilled expectation.

Trust and communication are super important.

Trust really comes from doing what you said you would. You can't earn the trust of a customer until they start doing business with you. Before that, it's all promises. The same can happen in a family. If the brother in charge of financial control of the company delivers a couple of years of excellent results – keeping costs under control and wisely setting aside reserves for a rainy day – he will then be trusted by the family to continue doing a good job, until he doesn't. The wayward nephew in charge of sales, who wines and dines his mates but can't close negotiations on critical projects, will lose the trust of the family – but without the right family charter rules, the family might not be able to exit him from that role without a major upset.

Family or business conflict

I see conflict as opportunity.

It's not that it is nice, but if you only see it as opposition, a difference of opinion or a point to 'draw a line in the sand' and defend your territory to the death, you might be missing a chance to learn from it.

You have probably heard the saying, 'If two people in a business agree all the time, one of them is irrelevant.'

Everyone brings something to the table. We all bring our experience, our skills, our viewpoints and our ideas. Sometimes, there is conflict over an idea or situation. I'd like you to consider that conflict as an opportunity to get the best outcome – this could be that you are right, or the other family member is right, or a fusion of your opinions and ideas might be even better, or you both may be wrong.

When I see conflict, I always take the stance, 'Okay, here is an opportunity.' It serves me well, and I'd encourage you to remember this the next time you see or are involved in a conflict. You may still be upset, angry, afraid, or feeling some other emotion, but if you can also step to the side and look for the opportunity, it will give you another tool for success.

> Conflict is inevitable; it doesn't have to end in trouble, a stalemate, a win-lose situation, or the end of a relationship.

Willingness and capability

Throughout the transition, success will depend on both generations being willing to explore each other's interests, capabilities and ideas. The younger generation cannot expect opportunities to be handed to them without effort or planning, and the older generation cannot assume that what worked for them will automatically suit the next.

In other words, keep the dialogue open. Ensure that willingness is matched with capability – on both sides.

For example, there may be willingness to explore a buy-out arrangement, but the capability to fund such a purchase might not yet exist. In this case, the family might need to consider options such as vendor financing, where the purchase is paid for from future profits. That's just one possibility of many that can arise in transition discussions.

Whatever the scenario, start with a shared willingness – then measure the capability.

This question of capability leads to another important factor in family business succession: complexity. These transitions are rarely straightforward, and often call for expertise beyond what exists within the family or the business.

At some point, both the family and the business will need external advisers – accountants, lawyers, financial planners and others – who can support, advise and walk the journey with you.

But it's vital not to lose sight of the family itself.

As a family business adviser, I know my limits. I'm not the person to give legal advice on trusts, family ownership structures or complex financial instruments. We may need additional expertise in areas such as valuation, intergenerational wealth transfer or governance. Sometimes we need support with people – including training and development.

I encourage families to be honest about their capability – individually and collectively – and to seek the right people for the right tasks when gaps appear.

Much of the professional advice needed during a transition is highly specialised and short term. It's not necessarily something a CEO or compliance-focused family accountant would have the background to handle. That's why, when I work with families on succession, I often help bring together a 'dream team' of legal, financial and structural experts to guide us through the process – with the goal of a successful outcome for everyone involved.

Other potential transition issues

What else is there to consider in a transition phase?

- **Lack of education and preparation for the next generation:** Without the right knowledge and mindset, future leaders may struggle to manage or grow the business effectively.
- **Cultural differences within the family:** As families expand and become more diverse, differing values around wealth, responsibility and authority can create tension.

- **Overlooking external influences:** Economic conditions, legal changes or societal expectations can impact the business if not considered in transition planning.
- **Failure to identify risks and opportunities early:** Focusing too narrowly may mean missing critical factors that could affect long-term success.
- **Inadequate planning for foreseeable challenges:** Assuming things will 'work out' can leave the family unprepared when difficulties inevitably arise.

Setting the business and the family up for success

My role is about prompting or asking the questions so that we can be as sure as possible we're making the right choices on ownership structure, business structure, legals, roles and responsibilities to set the business and the family up for success.[19]

In some cases, my experience has been that advisers such as accountants have advised a business owner on how to structure the business for tax purposes, but this decision has then led to unintended consequences for the family during the transition.

I'm going to come back to a metaphor I mentioned at the start of the book – the idea of a family tapestry. If you've ever been fortunate enough to see the Bayeux Tapestry, it tells the story of the conquest of England by William the Conqueror, Duke of Normandy. It is, in essence, a homage to a brother – William – probably by his half-brother Odo.

---

19 If you'd like some light reading or entertainment on the types of issues families can encounter during generational transition, I recommend the book *Family Wars*, the film *Crazy Rich Asians*, and the series *Succession*.

The tapestry is considered to be the finest record of the medieval period in England, including details of civil and military architecture and uniforms. It shows seafaring traditions and both real and imaginary animals and fables.

> If you think about your family, you are creating your own tapestry every day, every week, and every year.

While it might not be physically captured in something as beautiful as a tapestry, all the individual actions you take, the goals, wishes and dreams of family members, and the successes and failures are all occurring and could be – if someone was willing – captured in your family story.

As I mentioned at the start of the book, the front of the tapestry is what the world sees, and the back of the tapestry is only visible to the family. I know I said that the public will only see the beauty and not the chaos of the threads behind – the stitches, the knots, the mistakes and the dead ends – but in truth, there is beauty in the backside of the tapestry.

That is your true story, and you and your family will be the architects of it, in good times and bad. Choose the right threads, sew them into the right place, and you'll end up with a work of art.

Luke Newman is one client I recall with fondness. He didn't have a smooth journey, but a transition of sorts has occurred, and he is now in charge of a division of the family business that is performing exceptionally well.

The family didn't initially welcome his grand ideas of a touring show for the family business: Dracula's Restaurant. Yet through the facilitation of a family meeting, I was able to draw out underlying tensions and help the family find a way to accommodate Luke's vision.

He was able to secure both an increase in responsibility and remuneration, and in return, he brought this new vision to life, secured strong deals with iconic locations, and he has now overseen several years of taking the Dracula's Restaurant & Show concept to a whole new audience in different locations across Australia and the world.

Luke now has the power and position to lead this part of the business, and the overall business and the family are stronger as a result of the transition process.

Measuring success

As you progress through the transition, you are looking for the following outcomes and measures of success:

- The family will (or mostly will) be on the same page.
- Individuals will have their rightful place in the enterprise, should they choose to do so.
- All of the generations will be winning and have their aspirations met.
- There will be continued opportunity to meet as a family and, through the executives or board, see that the business is playing the investment role it needs to play for the family to achieve its goals of financial security and wealth creation and protection.
- Because communication is occurring, there is the opportunity to raise and think through issues, risks and opportunities.
- You are creating a better future together for the family and the business.

Transitions can be super complicated

'Transition' is a word that rolls off the tongue rather easily, but the reality of the transition process in business is that it can be super complicated.

You're unlikely to be able to navigate the transition of a family business of any reasonable size without outside help.

Why is that the case?

A transition will have a lot of moving parts.

On the business side, you are trying to move the business from the care and leadership of one generation of your family – usually Mum or Dad – into the care and leadership of someone (or more than one) from the next generation. You are dealing with different people, with different experiences, different skill sets, and potentially different generational viewpoints.

If you are the one taking over the business, are you as skilled at producing the product as your father? Do you understand the financial side of the business? Are you up to date on the technology used in the business? Are you as good a negotiator with suppliers or as good at servicing customers?

Beyond the people taking over various roles, you also have ownership issues to tackle in the transition. Do your parents have their own personal assets such as a house mortgage that has funded the business? Do you have enough capital behind you to buy them out? Or are they going to continue to own the business, while you run it?

You might have issues of changing consumer demand or changing technology needs of the business around the time of generational transition. Is the business growing, or does it need a new strategy to survive the next few decades under your ownership?

If you are in a generation taking over the business and there are multiple families involved, are there issues of ownership or shares for family members who are not going to work in the business? How will this be handled by you and the other siblings who are going to work in the business?

Then there is the issue of time. How long do you have? Are your parents wanting to get out sooner rather than later due to health issues or because they've had enough? Alternatively, is your mum or dad keen to keep working in the business even after you've taken over? How will this play out? Who is going to be making the decisions on the business then?

Are you going to be ready to take over the business when your father or mother retires, or will the business need a corporate leader from outside the family to hold the reins for a while, while you or your siblings get ready or gather skills and experience?

Do you even want to take over now that the time has come to consider transition?

Were you asked when you were younger if you wanted to take over the business, or is it just coming to a head now that Dad has decided he wants to move on?

In taking over a family business, you and your siblings may want to start considering the exit strategy now. Do you think you'd like to hand the business to your kids when they grow up? How do you see your life changing when you take over the business? Does it fit with your lifestyle choices?

What do your parents need and want when they step away from the business? Do they want a clean break, to stay on the board, or to keep ownership for a while? How much money do they need from the business to transition into retirement? Is that expectation even realistic based on the value of the business?

You can see there are so many factors in executing a transition, even with all the work you might have done as a family in the UNITE and BUILD stages.

There will never be a perfect time

The chances of you picking the perfect moment to transition the business for all concerned, the chances of the 'deal' being perfect for all concerned, the chances of you being perfectly ready to take over, of your parents being perfectly ready to step back, or the business being in perfect shape strategically at the time of transition, are pretty low.

But it doesn't have to be perfect. It just has to be workable and as good as it can be.

My point in emphasising all these complexities is that there is a lot you need to consider. It certainly isn't a case of picking a date and your mum and dad closing the shop one evening, then you opening up the next morning.

It's a little more complicated than that.

But you can prepare for a smooth transition.

It is a matter of taking the time, being diligent, raising, discussing and planning for the myriad issues of ownership, value, roles, structure, timing, strategy, and everything else.

Will it be perfect? No.

Can it be done as a win–win? Yes.

Where there is a will, there is a way.

Business transitions and estate planning

Speaking of wills, it can be important in this process to review your parents' will in the context of the business. In transitioning a business, your family's choices can affect and be affected by what your parents have decided in their will.

Is the business part of the will? Should the contents be discussed and adjusted based on what actions you are taking to transition the business while they are alive?

I've seen situations where the parents' will did not include anything about the business, and the death of a parent throws the transition into chaos as there is no agreement on what to do about various issues like ownership and roles. These are usually not covered in a will anyway, and often the parent who has been running the business does not write down or share everything in their head about the day-to-day running of the business.

Do the relevant wills contain information about family assets that are linked to the business, like the family home? How will that impact shareholdings in the business, or the need for funds to pay down debt from the parents that is linked to the business?

In one situation, a father had promised a business to one son – there were other siblings, but they were not part of the business 'deal'. The dad was supposed to have directed the accountant to write a letter to that effect saying that the son would take over the business. When push came to shove, it turned out the business accountant had done nothing, so the son was forced to seek his own advice and push his father to sign what had been agreed. There was upset involved, but eventually what occurred was that the son indeed took over, did well, and supported his mum and dad from the business over time.

How does health come into it? I've seen situations where, over time, the father or mother ends up with health issues like dementia. While there may have been verbal agreements prior to this point, does this health situation mean that those agreements aren't remembered, or aren't written down and can't be executed in a health emergency?

Older parents can pass away without plans being fully realised. When my father died, my mum took over and we had to battle our way through working out who was going to do what. It took time and energy because, in reality, my father was the only one who was across the entire business.

Some years ago, there was a very successful shoe business in Victoria. One evening, while flying his helicopter down to the Peninsula, the owner was killed in an accident in a storm. While there were other family members, no one was in a position to handle the business, and it did not survive long past the owner's death.

I'm not trying to be morbid, but we are not immortal as individuals, and to have a family business transition from one generation to another, we have to recognise that mortality and also manage the complexities of passing down the reins from one generation to another. Done right, our business can have some measure of immortality.

There is a sausage-making business in the UK that is still family-owned after about four hundred years – you can bet they have done the work, generation after generation, to pass down the reins of the business – from the family recipes to the business operations.

KPMG have recently released a report that says the average age of the family business owner is 65, so you can see this idea of transition is not a theoretical one. On average, every family business in Australia should be having these conversations, but often they are not.

In another report, it is suggested that several trillion dollars in assets are about to be passed from one generation to the next in Australia. Some of this will be in family businesses. If you're not having the conversations, you are not in control of this transfer of the business or the transition of the wealth. If you are not in control, if you don't have written agreements and plans, that control will rest somewhere else. It might lead to chaos between family members who have no direction and agreement and spend time arguing over their rights and what they should receive. In the worst case, it ends up as a trustee issue, and the family ends up with no control over the family business or wealth.

KPMG also mentioned in their report that the ATO knows what is going on. You might think you're running a quiet family business and going about your own affairs. But they know what you are doing; they know what you are spending your business's money on and the cars and horses you might be buying. It might be in all of this that your mum and dad can't sell the business, don't want to sell the business, or there is nothing to sell as the business is too tied up with their personal assets and home.

Will the bank of Mum and Dad be exposed by the demands of transition?

You just don't know.

If you have multiple family members, each of you will have your own asset and tax position, and each of you could be influenced differently by that position in the event of a transition of shares or ownership in a business.

Time to TRANSITION

It is not a simple handover of the keys. There is a lot more to it, and as such, you have to take the time to ask the right questions and find the right answers to these questions for each member of your family and for the business.

The following image shows why timing can be such a challenge. This chart illustrates the evolving needs and engagement of parents and children in a family business over time. As the parents' role and influence peak and begin to decline, the children's involvement and responsibilities increase. The parents' needs shift from security to a desire for freedom and legacy, while the children's early need for guidance evolves into a need for autonomy and opportunity. The diagram highlights the delicate crossover point – prior to estate transfer – when aligning these changing needs is crucial to ensure a smooth and successful succession.

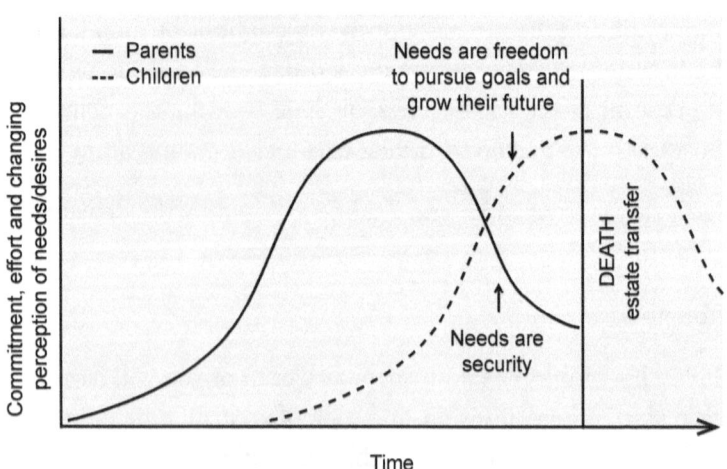

In the transition phase, you're looking at financial capital, but importantly you are also looking at human capital. Who is going to work in the business? What role will they have? How will the family's interests be protected over time? How do we keep the show on the road? Do we want to keep the show on the road?

I'd like to add that plans are important, but once you've done your plan, for heaven's sake, don't let it sit in a drawer to gather dust.

> A good transition might take years, so come back to the plan regularly and track how you are progressing on the various key strategies you need to put in place.

How are the finances being handled? How is the structure and ownership being managed? Who is working in the business and how are their skill sets aligning with the roles they are playing? Plan your work, and work your plan.

A family business is a vehicle to generate wealth, but never forget it is also a vehicle for opportunity to develop individual family members. The business might support education or skills development. Family members may go out into the world with the aim of developing skills that can be brought back into the family business at some point. A family business can support the education of future generations. A family business, through a foundation, can provide support to charities or causes that are close to the family's heart.

I've seen instances where younger generations can be exposed to the work of the family business by getting involved in choosing charities for the family business to support. They become attuned to the philanthropy of the business and then grow into a role within the business over time.

Transitioning a family business can be complex, difficult and challenging, and it can take time. You will never get it perfect, but the result can be highly rewarding for all involved. *Progress* is your catchword, not *perfection*.

I've been asked many times over the years when is a good time to start teaching the kids about the family business. The answer is there is no right time, but there is also no wrong time. Sooner is better than later.

Go home tonight and ask your kids about your business. Something like, 'What business do you think your mum or dad is in?'

You might be surprised.

One client's kids drew butterflies when their dad asked this question. They were young.

But equally, I remember sitting on my Poppa's knee in a little golf cart going around our factory, and even those early exposures to our family business left an impression on me. Do you remember the first time you took an interest in your dad or mum's business? The first time you worked in it? Maybe during school holidays?

A proper transition in a business may take many years. Start as early as you need and use the time wisely. Get a family business adviser who can ask the right questions to guide you on your journey.

Let's say your family is working towards a transition, and the unthinkable happens: the family member who owns and runs the business is hit by a bus. Here are two questions that might prompt you to consider why transition is so important:

- Who *would* open the business up tomorrow if this happens?
- Who *should* open the business tomorrow?

If the answers to these two questions are different, how do you decide?

Exercise: Navigating the TRANSITION

If you've reached the TRANSITION phase, you've already put in significant work. Now it's time to bring everything together and prepare for the successful transfer of leadership, ownership and stewardship to the next generation.

This stage is less about decisions made in isolation, and more about ensuring clarity, alignment and communication across generations.

1. What are the biggest concerns or questions your family still has about the transition?

   ....
   ....
   ....
   ....
   ....
   ....
   ....

2. Who currently owns the business, and who will own it in the future? Are you clear on how this transfer will occur?

   ....
   ....
   ....
   ....
   ....
   ....
   ....

3. What roles will each family member play during and after the transition? Has this been agreed?

4. What external advisers (e.g. accountant, lawyer, governance coach) are you working with – or need to work with – to support the transition?

5. Reflect: What does a 'successful transition' look like for you, your family and the business?

A FINAL WORD FROM JOHN

YOUR LEGACY

'It is only when we develop others that we permanently succeed.'
Harvey S Firestone, founder of Firestone Tire & Rubber Company and pioneer of industrial innovation through people

I'm going to admit something to you.

I don't like the word *legacy*.

When I hear people talk about legacy, I sometimes cringe inside.

My truth is that you won't be the one to know what your legacy is because you'll already be gone. What I do know is that creating a lasting impact means making the right decisions and doing the right things *today*.

Whether you're part of the generation handing the business over, or the generation taking the reins, you have a part to play in ensuring success for everyone involved.

I believe you want to protect and preserve the family dynamic as the first and foremost goal. No one should be left wondering when their time will come. No one should be forced to participate in the family business if they don't want to. No one should be left in a position where they have the responsibility but not the character, skills or resources to get the job done. No one should be allowed to shirk either their duty to the family or their responsibility to the business.

I believe legacy will be created if you just do the right things and make the right decisions from these viewpoints:

- Everyone is on their own individual journey and has their own interests, talents and aspirations.
- Everyone in your family wants to be secure and wants to pursue their dreams and goals.
- A family is a great place to set up the next generation to at least have the opportunity to be healthy, wealthy and wise.
- A family with strong values and a strong charter can be a strong foundation for a business.
- A family business is an investment vehicle, but it requires the right purpose, the right engine, the right resources and the right people to ensure it achieves the purpose the family has for that investment.
- For a business to transition through multiple generations, it has to continue to have a reason to exist and needs the family to be strong and aligned to be good stewards of that business over time.

- Family and business have different goals, and separating them is as important as understanding the points at which they intersect.

I started this book talking about how much I love family business.

It is ingrained in my DNA and in my life's purpose.

As a young boy, I sat next to my grandfather in a golf buggy while he practised MBWA – Management by Walking Around. I saw him take advantage of opportunities to pivot the business as market conditions changed. I saw my father rush home to farewell my grandfather when he died unexpectedly. I worked with my father as he stamped his own indelible mark on the business, and as my uncle and he sold parts of the business and transitioned once again.

I grew up, learnt the business, and then contributed to the operational excellence of the business my father ran. I had ideas but had to operate within the boundaries of my father's control of that business.

When he died, I had expectations of taking over, which wasn't to be in the immediate aftermath of his passing. Yet, I did eventually buy the business from family and transition it again and again.

You are on a journey that I know very well. From within and without, through the fortune of being a family business adviser for many decades and working with many families just like yours.

I encourage you to take the steps I've outlined in this book. Take them in order or as needed according to your situation. But take them nonetheless. Invest the time in communication and developing shared understanding and your family will thrive.

By taking the three steps of UNITE, BUILD and TRANSITION, I believe any family can use a business to achieve their financial security and wealth goals over many generations.

As you continue on your journey to navigate your transition, I wish you bon voyage and encourage you to reach out if I can do anything further to guide you and your family on this journey.

I look forward to the opportunity for this conversation to continue and raise a glass to your success, now and in the future.

To family!

APPENDIX

WORKBOOK
if you were hit by a bus

What happens to your business if you're not there tomorrow?

This appendix is about the future of your family business in the event of your death.

Many people who work through these questions find them both challenging and confronting. That, unfortunately, is the reality of planning for the unexpected death of the leader of a family business.

If you find the questions difficult to answer, let me assure you: your family will find them considerably more so – especially if they are forced to deal with them without your guidance during what will likely be a very emotional period.

For their sake, and for the future of your family business, please give this the attention it deserves.

If you were hit by a bus today ...

- Who *would* go into the business tomorrow and keep things running?

  ....
  ....

- Who *should* go into the business and keep things running?

  ....
  ....

- If those are two different people, what have you put in place to ensure the right person takes over?

  ....
  ....
  ....
  ....

- Who, besides you, can access the business's money?

  ....
  ....

- What checks and balances are in place to ensure that bills and suppliers are paid – and not the individual accessing the funds?

  ....
  ....
  ....
  ....
  ....

- Does the bank have authorisation to allow that person access to the account?

- Is that authorisation voided by your death (e.g. due to dual signature rules)?

- Who else knows the access codes and passwords to essential functions, such as:
    - Internet banking
    - Key websites
    - Domain registration
    - Social media accounts
    - Supplier portals

- Is there a safe?

- Who knows where the safe is?

- Who knows the combination or how to access it?

- Where are the spare keys for the following stored, and who knows where they are?
    - Plant/equipment
    - Storage areas
    - Safes
    - Company vehicles

    ....
    ....

- Are there any contracts in place that would no longer be valid in your absence?

    ....
    ....
    ....
    ....

- What personal guarantees have you provided in connection with the business?

    ....
    ....
    ....
    ....

- What would happen to those guarantees if you were no longer around?

    ....
    ....
    ....
    ....

- Could a financier repossess assets if you are not available to manage the business?

- What intellectual property (IP) is legally registered and owned by you and/or the company?
  (For example: trademarks, patents, designs, copyrights)

- Where is the documentation that proves ownership of the IP?

- What licences are in place where you are the licensee or licensor?

- How much business-critical IP is stored only in your head?

- What are you doing (or what have you done) to capture that knowledge?

- Who are the following key people in your affairs?
    - Executor
    - Lawyer
    - Accountant
    - Banker (personal)
    - Banker (business)
    - Financial Planner
    - Insurance Broker

- Are there any secrets – personal or business-related – that could cause issues or surprises?

- Who knows about these matters?

- Do you have a letter marked 'Open only after my death'?

- Where is that letter kept?

- Who is the person you truly want to take over your business?

- Do they know this?

- Has documentation been prepared to give them authority?

- Where is that documentation kept?

- Are copies of all crucial documents filed off-site?

- Where are those off-site copies stored?

- Would your answers to any of these questions change if you were incapacitated but still alive?

- Do you have an enduring power of attorney in place?

- Has the nominated person signed the document?

- Do they know where it is stored?

- Do you have a safe deposit box?

- Who knows where it is located?

- Do you have a valid, up-to-date will?

- Does your executor know where to find your will?

- Have you documented your funeral preferences?

- Have you discussed those preferences with your family?

- Where are the answers to these questions written down?

- Who else knows where that documentation is kept?

Questions for yourself

- Do I have a written plan?

- Who knows where it is?

- Is your plan consistent with your will?

- Is it complete, up-to-date and communicated to all those involved?

- What do I want to happen at a family level regarding the future of the business?

- What do I want to happen at a business level regarding the operation of the business?

- Will the business continue to provide an income for my spouse and dependents?

- Does the plan treat all children fairly and equitably, especially when not involved in the business?

Conversations with family

- Who is covered by the plan?

- Do they understand the plan?

- Do they agree with the plan?

- If there is disagreement with the plan, why?

- Do they have a clear vision of the future of the business?

- Does the successor have the skills to operate the business?

- Do they want to operate the business?

- What consequential staff changes must be made?

- Can they maintain the economic viability of the existing business?

- Will it be necessary to make changes for the continued economic viability of the business?

- Does the plan treat all children fairly and equally with provision made for children not working in the business?

Conversations with your business partner(s)

- Is there a person(s) with the appropriate authority (in writing) to take charge of the day-to-day operations of the business?

- Have you given any guarantees that will be affected by your sudden demise?

- Is there any effect on banking? Are other signatories needed?

Conversations with your lawyer

- Do you have a will and is it current?

  ....

  ....

- Do you understand probate and how it may affect your estate?

  ....

  ....

- Have you set up any trusts?

  ....

  ....

- Have you considered how estate disputes might be avoided?

  ....

  ....

- Do you have an enduring power of attorney in place?

  ....

  ....

- Have you assigned enduring guardianship?

  ....

  ....

Checklist for executors and attorneys

- [ ] Key contact details of your solicitor, accountant, financial adviser and insurance broker
- [ ] Location of will and contact details of executors, location and details of insurance policies
- [ ] Location of power of attorney (if real estate is involved, is it registered?)
- [ ] Details of all bank accounts and credit cards. Access and passwords to key functions
- [ ] Loans, assets, stocks and shares, combination/location of the key to the safe
- [ ] Pensions, property owned (sole, joint, mortgages)
- [ ] Leases, partnership agreement, trademarks, patents, designs, copyrights, licences
- [ ] Memberships, any other important information
- [ ] Include names and all contact details where appropriate

Conversations with your financial planner

- Do you have an estate plan that includes both estate and non-estate assets?

- Have you considered tax-effective strategies for distributing your estate?

- Have you made arrangements for superannuation, life insurance proceeds, and family trust assets?

- Do you understand the tax implications of inherited property or shares?

- Have you made provisions for beneficiaries who receive Centrelink benefits?

- Do you wish to create a testamentary trust for children or other dependents?

WHY WORK WITH A FAMILY BUSINESS ADVISER?

Family and business don't always mix easily.

But with the right guidance, they absolutely can.

For over 40 years, John Broons has helped family businesses navigate the tricky intersections of communication, legacy and leadership. Through robust, honest conversations, he helps families align their vision and strengthen trust across generations.

The result?

Better business outcomes.

Clearer roles.

A stronger sense of unity.

If your family business needs support with succession planning, conflict resolution or simply building a healthier dynamic, John brings experience, compassion and a steady hand.

Let's make your family business work for everyone involved.

Visit **www.johnbroons.com** to learn more.

THE SIX-MONTH PROGRAM FOR SMALL FAMILY BUSINESSES

Future-proof your family business

Some families in business feel harmony and purpose.

Others feel tension and uncertainty.

Most? Somewhere in between.

In this six-month program, John Broons works closely with small family businesses to create clarity, improve communication and prepare for the future. His practical, no-nonsense approach helps families make real progress – without dodging the hard conversations.

Whether you're preparing for succession or just trying to avoid a family blow-up at Christmas lunch, this program gives you the tools to move forward together.

It's not just business – it's personal. And it's worth getting right.

Enquire now at **www.johnbroons.com**.

THE 12-MONTH PROGRAM FOR LARGE FAMILY BUSINESSES

Leadership, legacy and long-term thinking

The stakes are higher in large family businesses.

And no one understands that better than John Broons.

With decades of experience guiding complex family enterprises, John helps families shift from assumptions and avoidance to alignment and action. His 12-month program is designed for those ready to tackle the real issues – succession, leadership, communication and continuity.

What you'll get:

- Independent facilitation of the tough conversations.
- Long-term strategic alignment.
- Clarity on roles, responsibilities and vision.
- Greater stability and trust between generations.

Your family business deserves more than survival. It deserves a thriving legacy.

Connect with John today at **www.johnbroons.com**.

INDIVIDUAL COACHING

In one-on-one coaching sessions with John Broons, you'll have a safe space where you focus entirely on you, your role, your challenges and your goals. John will:

- help you unpack what's going on
- offer practical strategies
- guide you toward greater clarity and confidence
- teach you how to navigate the emotionally charged issues that must be addressed in family business
- ask the right questions
- challenge assumptions
- encourage honest reflection.

Difficult topics become easier to approach, and what once felt stuck begins to shift.

John's coaching helps you build trust within your family, clarify your responsibilities, and contribute to a stronger, more united business. If you're ready for meaningful change, individual coaching with John is the place to start.

IF YOU'RE LOOKING FOR A SPEAKER ...

When John Broons takes the stage, audiences are immediately drawn in by his warmth, authenticity and storytelling prowess. With over 40 years of working inside the world of family business, John delivers keynotes that are both insightful and deeply relatable. He shares real stories from the trenches – the triumphs, the tensions and the turning points – bringing to life the complex world of family enterprises. His presentations offer more than just theory; they provide practical tools and a fresh perspective on leadership, succession, and navigating family dynamics in business.

Audiences leave with a renewed sense of possibility, are inspired to act, and are equipped with strategies to protect their legacy for future generations. If you're looking for a speaker who brings wisdom, humour and real impact, John Broons delivers.

Call John on **0433 131 070** or email **john@johnbroons.com**.

www.ingramcontent.com/pod-product-compliance
Lightning Source LLC
Chambersburg PA
CBHW030325080526
44584CB00012B/715